U0123938

Development Report on Zhejiang-Czech Economic and Trade Cooperation under the Framework of the Belt and Road Initiative

(2020)

Zhou Junzi, Zheng Yali, Zhang Haiyan, Hu Wenjing

Translated by

Xu Lei, Fan Shuangshuang, Lyu Fangyi, Zhuo Jiani

ZHEJIANG UNIVERSITY PRESS
浙江大学出版社

Preface

Zhejiang is the pioneer of local cooperation between China and Central and Eastern European Countries (CEECs). In terms of trade, the total trade volume between Zhejiang and 17 Central and Eastern European countries in 2019 was nearly 100 billion yuan. Compared with the establishment of Cooperation between China and Central and Eastern European Countries in 2012, the trade volume has doubled, accounting for 15% of the total trade volume between China and Central and Eastern European Countries. In terms of investment, there are many successful cases of companies in the high-tech industry working together to explore the Eurasian market. And "going abroad" presents a gratifying change in which high-tech enterprises are increasingly gathering and the main business of investment is increasingly clear. For example, in the Czech Republic, the investment projects of Wanxiang Group, XZB Tech Co., Ltd., Hamaton Automotive Technology Co., Ltd., and Minth Group in Zhejiang all focus on their pillar industries in the field of automobile manufacturing. The Czech Republic is the leader in economic development among CEECs and has a developed industrial civilization. The *2020 Global Manufacturing Index* shows that the Czech Republic is the most suitable European country for developing manufacturing, while the *Global Competitiveness Report 2020* shows that the Czech Republic is the most competitive country in Central and Eastern Europe. In recent years, in terms of cooperation with the Czech Republic, Zhejiang has made great efforts in platform construction, project promotion and people-to-people exchanges, showing a positive momentum of frequent high-level visits, active two-way investment and trade, and active participation of enterprises, cities and counties. Facing the COVID-19, Zhejiang has actively acted and taken the responsibility to jointly fight against the pandemic with the Czech Republic.

2

Development Report on Zhejiang-Czech Economic and Trade
Cooperation under the Framework of the Belt and Road Initiative (2020)

With the mission of "an important window", Zhejiang and the Czech Republic have continuously enriched the connotation of cooperation.

The *Development Report on Zhejiang-Czech Economic and Trade Cooperation under the Framework of the Belt and Road Initiative (2020)* summarizes the current situation of cooperation between Zhejiang and the Czech Republic, and focuses on the development trend of Czech economy and key industries. The report is divided into three parts. Part 1 "Current Situation" presents the import and export trade in 2019, two-way investment, people-to-people exchanges and joint anti-pandemic fight between Zhejiang and the Czech Republic. Among them, the case of Hamaton Automotive Technology Co., Ltd. acquiring Westfalia Metal Hoses Group is selected as the example of the two-way investment, which illustrates the potential and benefits of Zhejiang-Czech cooperation under the framework of the Belt and Road Initiative; the joint anti-pandemic section reviews the joint efforts of China (Zhejiang) and the Czech Republic to fight the pandemic, and expresses the confidence in deepening practical cooperation and enhancing the friendship between the two sides. Part 2 "Development" summarizes the economic development of the Czech Republic in 2019 and forecasts the economic development trend of the Czech Republic, providing decision-making references for enterprises and institutions interested in carrying out economic and trade cooperation with the Czech Republic. According to the report, Czech domestic market segments are facing the challenge of the weakening of both supply and demand and difficulties in this stage of development. The duration of the pandemic and the effectiveness of policy responses are to be critical variables. Part 3 "Feature" takes Czech manufacturing industry as the analysis object, which is divided into two parts. The first part makes a comprehensive analysis of the development status of Czech manufacturing industry from the dimensions of scale status, industry characteristics, international market dependence and digital development. The second part looks forward to the future, summarizing the development advantages and development difficulties of Czech manufacturing industry. Based on this, the report makes research and gets a certain judgment on the development situation of Czech manufacturing industry from the short-term and medium and long-term perspectives.

This report is released in Chinese, English and Czech. Zhou Junzi is responsible for the framework design and overall draft review as well as the writing of part of the "Current Situation" and the "Development"; Zheng Yali is in charge of the organization of composing and draft review as well as writing part of the "Feature"; Zhang Haiyan is responsible for the research guidance and draft review, and writes part of the "Current Situation"; Hu Wenjing writes part of the "Feature". Xu Lei is responsible for the organization of English translation and overall draft review; Xu Lei, Lyu Fangyi and Zhuo Jiani are responsible for the translation of the "Current Situation"; Xu Lei and Fan Shuangshuang are responsible for the translation of the "Development"; Fan Shuangshuang, Zhuo Jiani and Lyu Fangyi are responsible for the translation of the "Feature". Xu Weizhu is responsible for the organization of Czech translation and overall draft review; Xu Weizhu and her team are responsible for the translation of the "Development", and for the draft review of the "Current Situation" and the "Feature"; Renata Čuhlová is responsible for the translation of the "Current Situation" and the "Feature". With this report as a medium, we hope to encourage discussions and exchanges with the Czech Republic and the Belt and Road researchers around the globe to promote scientific research cooperation and work in unity to contribute and harvest fruitful research results.

This report is the annual research result of the Czech Research Center of Zhejiang Financial College, which is established under the guidance of the Ministry of Education of China. The Czech Center is a regional research center, an open research platform dedicated to the comprehensive study of Czech politics, economy, culture and society as well as a new type of think tank serving the needs of the Belt and Road construction.

The impact of COVID-19 in 2020 delayed the release of this research report. Due to the limitations of the research team, improprieties are unavoidable, and we are open to all sectors of society for criticism and improvement.

Zheng Yali

President, Zhejiang Financial College
Director, Czech Research Center

Contents

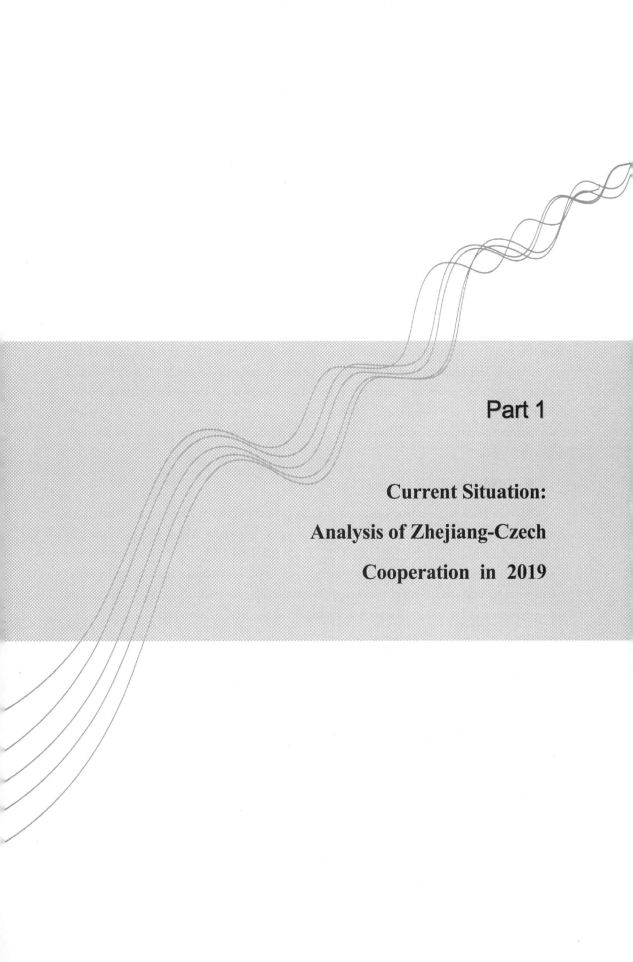

Part 1

Current Situation:

Analysis of Zhejiang-Czech

Cooperation in 2019

2

Development Report on Zhejiang-Czech Economic and Trade
Cooperation under the Framework of the Belt and Road Initiative (2020)

Introduction

◆ Trade

In 2019, the total Zhejiang-Czech trade volume exceeded USD 1 billion, among which Zhejiang's export to the Czech Republic reached USD 862 million while its import from the Czech Republic amounted to USD 146 million, indicating an expanding trade surplus. Regarding the commodity composition, Zhejiang mainly exported garments, textile, electrical wires and cables, etc., to the Czech Republic, with the export of storage batteries increased by more than four times driven by investment. Mechanical and electrical products, raw materials and resource-based products were mostly imported from the Czech Republic with an obvious growth in auto parts and logs. Regarding the main trading bodies, exporters to the Czech Republic in Zhejiang were mainly private enterprises, among which cross-border e-commerce and other new foreign trade forms were playing increasingly important roles.

◆ Investment

2019 did not witness many new investment projects between Zhejiang and the Czech Republic except for the representative acquisition of Westfalia Metal Hoses Group by Hamaton Automotive Technology Co., Ltd., which involved 1/3 of its transaction amount with Czech Business Company. The merger case not only constituted a major asset restructuring, but also brought synergy effects such as resource integration, brand superposition and international layout to Hamaton in the field of auto parts.

◆ People-to-People Exchanges

2019 coincided with the 70th anniversary of the establishment of diplomatic relations between China and the Czech Republic, the Year of Education and Youth Exchange between China and Central and Eastern European Countries. Zhejiang actively explored diverse forms of cultural exchanges with the Czech Republic. The education cooperation platform was actively built to expand the development space. The tourism boom cooled down, and the speed of growth turned from rising to falling. Cultural exchanges displayed ongoing diversity, building a bridge connecting people on both sides.

◆ Joint-efforts-to-fight-against-pandemic Analysis

At the beginning of 2020, COVID-19 spread across the whole world. Since the emergence of confirmed cases in the Czech Republic, the Czech Republic has responded promptly with well-targeted policies and undergone three stages, namely the spreading period, the outbreak period and the controlled period. In the battle against COVID-19, China (Zhejiang) acted actively and assisted in fighting against the virus with the Czech Republic. During the post-pandemic period, it is entirely possible for Zhejiang to take missionary responsibilities to give full play to Zhejiang enterprises, overseas Chinese and open platforms. It will work as an "important bridge" to promote the vibrant cooperation between Zhejiang and the Czech Republic.

4

Development Report on Zhejiang-Czech Economic and Trade
Cooperation under the Framework of the Belt and Road Initiative (2020)

The Czech Republic is an important node country for Zhejiang to get deeply involved in the construction of the Belt and Road Initiative and "17+1 Cooperation". In 2019, the two sides jointly ushered in a new phase of cooperation. In terms of trade, the volume of Zhejiang-Czech imports and exports reached USD 1.008 billion, an increase of 8.2% over the same period last year. In terms of investment, the newly added merger and acquisition projects involved auto parts, the pillar industry of the Czech Republic, with an investment amount exceeding USD 100 million. In terms of people-to-people exchanges, the educational cooperation mode is constantly innovating and expanding. Diverse cultural and artistic exchange activities have been conducted. In terms of fighting against COVID-19, China (Zhejiang) and the Czech Republic have enhanced friendship and cooperation, injecting new impetus to further practical cooperation between the two sides.

Ⅰ. Trade

1. Overview

The trade volume between the two countries reached a new record high, exceeding USD 1 billion for the first time, but the overall scale was limited and the trade surplus showed a remarkable expansion.

In 2019, the trade volume between Zhejiang and the Czech Republic reached a new record high, exceeding USD 1 billion, a year-on-year increase of 8.2%, 4.8% higher than the growth rate over the same period. Within this period, Zhejiang exported USD 862 million to the Czech Republic, a year-on-year increase of 8.4%. Imports from the Czech Republic reached USD 146 million, a year-on-year increase of 7.1%. Looking back over the past decade, the import and export trade between Zhejiang and the Czech Republic showed a good growth trend, especially in recent five years. As shown in Figure 1-1, from 2010 to 2019, the bilateral trade volume increased from USD 573 million to USD 1.008 billion, with an average annual growth rate of 6.5% among which Zhejiang's exports to the Czech

Republic increased from USD 489 million to USD 862 million, an average annual growth rate of 6.5%. Imports from the Czech Republic increased from USD 84 million to USD 146 million, an average annual increase of 6.3%. On the whole, the import and export trade between Zhejiang and Czech developed rapidly, but the overall scale was limited with the trade surplus showed a remarkable expansion.

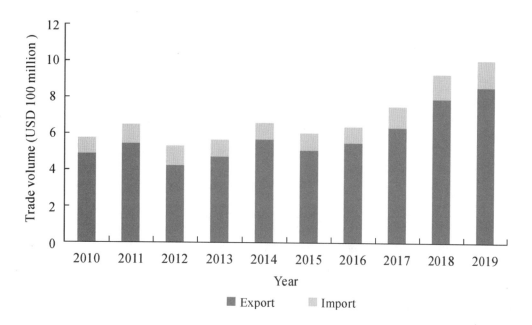

Figure 1-1   Trade Volume of Zhejiang-Czech Imports and Exports from 2010 to 2019

(**Source:** Department of Commerce of Zhejiang Province)

2. Commodity Composition

Zhejiang commodities exported to the Czech Republic were mainly garments and textile, electric wires and cables, etc., with the export of storage batteries increased by more than four times driven by investment. On the other hand, imported commodities from the Czech Republic were primarily mechanical and electrical products, raw materials and resource-based products with a remarkable growth in auto parts and logs.

In regards to the composition of export commodities, the top ten Zhejiang exports to the Czech Republic in 2019 were shown in Figure 1-2, with apparel and garment accessories, electric wires and cables as the major commodities. Of all the Zhejiang exports to the Czech Republic, apparel and garment accessories were the principal products, with the export amount of USD 97.2887 million, contributing to 11.3% of total exports in 2019. Among them, garments and clothing accessories ranked first in export commodities, with an export value of USD 69.2959 million. Textile yarns, fabrics and made-up articles ranked second in export commodities, with an export value of USD 27.9928 million, followed by electric wires and cables, electric motors and generators, batteries, valued less than USD 30 million, showing a large gap compared with textile and garment.

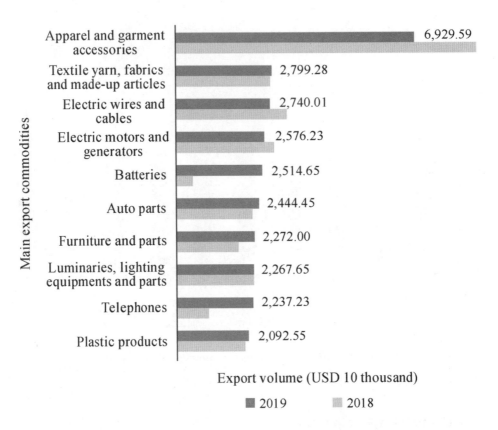

Figure 1-2   Scale and a Year-on-Year Growth or Reduction of Major Zhejiang Commodities Exported to the Czech Republic in 2019

(**Source:** Department of Commerce of Zhejiang Province)

By vertical comparison, among the top ten major commodities exported to the Czech Republic in 2019, batteries manifested the sharpest increase, achieving a 426.2% rise, followed by telephones with a year-on-year increase of 144.0%. The largest decline was in the export of garment and clothing accessories, a year-on-year decrease of 20.8%, followed by electric wires and cables, electric motors and generators, which dropped by 15.2% and 10.1% respectively. These three categories of products ranked as the top three export commodities in 2018, with an increase of more than 30.0% in that year. Since Zhejiang's main export commodities to the Czech Republic were limited in scale and mostly concentrated within several certain enterprises so that they were easy to be fluctuated by the expansion or reduction of the business scale of some certain enterprises. For example, Wangxiang A123 Systems Co., Ltd. invested and set up a lithium battery factory in the Czech Republic, which was the drive of export increase of related products, the main reason of a sharp increase of battery exports to the Czech Republic.

With regards to import, the top ten commodities of Zhejiang imported from the Czech Republic in 2019 were shown in Figure 1-3. Scrap metal and metal processing machine tools were the main products. The top ten import commodities of Zhejiang from the Czech Republic accounted for 55.1% of Zhejiang's total imports from the Czech Republic over the same period. The commodity concentration rate was higher than that of the main exported products (33.5%), and it was also higher than the overall concentration rate of the main imports in Zhejiang (41.0%) over the same period. To a certain extent, it reflected Zhejiang's main demanding areas of commodities from the Czech Republic. The total import volume of machine tools for metal processing, auto parts, diodes and similar semiconductor devices reached USD 44.5442 million, accounting for 30.4% of Zhejiang's total imports from the Czech Republic. The total import volume of raw materials and resource-based products such as scrap metal, logs and plastics in primary forms reached USD 29,265,500, accounting for 20.0% of Zhejiang's total imports from the Czech Republic.

By vertical comparison, among the top ten major commodities imported from the Czech Republic in 2019, logs showed the largest growth rate, a seven times year-on-year increase. This is mainly due to the acceleration of local timber logging and trade volume caused by forest pests in the Czech Republic, the imposition of customs duties on imported broad-leaved timber from the United States as well as the continued cessation of natural forest logging in China. According to the data of CnWood (www.cnwood.cn) in 2019, the Czech Republic ranked among the top five countries in terms of log import to China. In addition, Zhejiang's imports of auto parts from the Czech Republic showed a two times year-on-year increase. With a large-scale complete industrial chain, automobile industry has always been the pillar industry of Czech economy. In terms of auto parts, Ernst & Young, a European investment monitoring institution, rated Czech as the world's best investment destination for the auto parts industry for many years. In recent years, Zhejiang's import of auto parts from the Czech Republic has shown a good momentum, complementing the domestic auto parts industry to some extent, and is also conducive to the improvement of quality and efficiency of auto products.

8

Development Report on Zhejiang-Czech Economic and Trade
Cooperation under the Framework of the Belt and Road Initiative (2020)

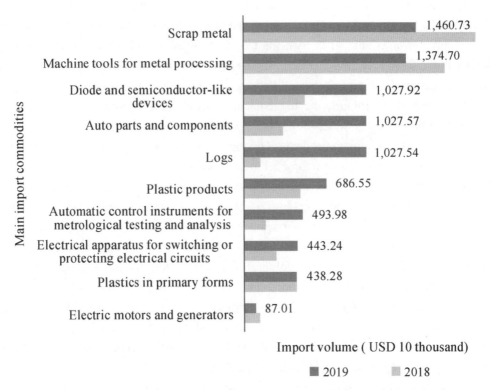

**Figure 1-3   Scale and Year-on-Year Growth or Reduction of Major Commodities
Imported from the Czech Republic to Zhejiang in 2019**

(**Source:** Department of Commerce of Zhejiang Province)

3. Main Trading Bodies

**Private enterprises account for a relatively high proportion, while cross-border
e-commerce and other new foreign trade forms play a more prominent role.**

In terms of the export trade scale, the top 20 export enterprises of Zhejiang Province,
China to the Czech Republic in 2019 were Mobiwire Mobiles (Ningbo) Co., Ltd., Panasonic
Motor (Hangzhou) Co., Ltd., Wanxiang A123 Systems Co., Ltd., Zhejiang Cfmoto Power
Co., Ltd., Wanxiang Import & Export Co., Ltd., Zhejiang Ke'en Sanitary Fixtures Co., Ltd.,
Hangzhou Hikvision Digital Technology Co., Ltd., Cixi Donggong Electric Co., Ltd.,
Hangzhou Sunrise Technology Co., Ltd., DENSO（Hangzhou）Co., Ltd., Zhejiang Zhaolong
Cable Co., Ltd., Ningbo Daye Garden Machinery Co., Ltd., Zhejiang Huahai Pharmaceutical
Co., Ltd., Nidec Shibaura (Zhejiang) Co., Ltd., Ningbo Timberword International Trade Co.,
Ltd., Welfull Group Co., Ltd., Express E-commerce Package (8639), Ningbo Haitian
International Co., Ltd., China-Base Ningbo Foreign Trade Co., Ltd., Haining Hisener Trade
Co., Ltd.

In terms of the business nature, private enterprises played a major role in Zhejiang's exports to the Czech Republic, accounting for nearly half of the top 20 enterprises exported from Zhejiang to the Czech Republic. From the perspective of main products, it mainly involved electronic equipment, motors, lithium batteries, auto parts, etc. Regarding to the business model, with the continuous promotion of Czech Station construction project, cross-border e-commerce plays an increasingly role in Zhejiang's export to the Czech Republic.

In terms of the import trade scale, the top 20 enterprises importing from the Czech Republic to Zhejiang Province, China in 2019 included Lego Toy Manufacturing (Jiaxing) Co., Ltd., Ningbo Leadgo E-commerce Co., Ltd., Jiashan Sunking Power Equipment Technology Co., Ltd., Ningbo Jintian Copper (Group) Co., Ltd., Asia Euro Automobile Manufacturing (Taizhou) Co., Ltd., Zhejiang Material Industry Civil Products & Blasting Equipment Co., Ltd., Haitian Plastics Machinery Co., Ltd., Zhejiang Material Industry Senhua Group Co., Ltd., Tederic Machinery Co., Ltd., Joyson (Huzhou) Automotive Safety Systems Co., Ltd., Hailun Piano Co., Ltd., Hangzhou Steam Turbine Co., Ltd., KSK Automotive Components (Pinghu) Co., Ltd., China Petrochemical International (Ningbo) Co., Ltd., Kayaku Safety Systems (Huzhou) Co., Ltd., Zhejiang Neoglory Jewelry Co., Ltd., Zhejiang Scientific Instruments & Materials Import / Export Co., Ltd., Hangzhou Xinye Lid Manufacturing Co., Ltd., Zhejiang Liuqiao Industrial Co., Ltd., Ningbo Kangshida Import & Export Co., Ltd.

In terms of the business nature, the top 20 Zhejiang enterprises imported from the Czech Republic included 9 private enterprises, more than that of 2018. From the perspective of new enterprises, compared with 2018, in 2019, among the top 20 enterprises that imported from the Czech Republic, 10 were new, engaged in businesses of auto parts, metal processing, scientific equipment and other fields, consistent with the advantageous industries of the Czech Republic. From the perspective of business model, the status of cross-border e-commerce in Zhejiang's import from the Czech Republic has been continuously improved. For example, the import scale ranking of Ningbo Leadgo E-commerce Co., Ltd. rose from 8th in 2018 to 2nd in 2019.

II. Investment

In 2019, the new two-way investment between Zhejiang and the Czech Republic was limited. According to the data of the Department of Commerce of Zhejiang Province, in 2019, two investment projects in the Czech Republic were newly approved, with a Chinese investment filing amount of USD 22.2866 million, mainly investing in manufacturing industries of automobile, computer, communication and other electronic equipments. Among them, one of the large-scale new investment projects was the acquisition of

Westfalia Metal Hoses Group (WMHG) by Hamaton Automotive Technology Co., Ltd. (Hamaton). The details of the case are as follows.

1. Enterprise Profile

Established in 1993, Hamaton Automotive Technology Co., Ltd. is a professional manufacturer engaged in research and development (R&D), production and sales of tire valves, tire pressure monitoring systems (TPMS) and related tools and accessories. In the automotive aftermarket (AM market), it cooperates closely with after-sales service providers such as 31 Inc., Tyresure and REMA. In the original equipment manufacturer market (OEM market), Hamaton has established a long-term and stable cooperation with first-class suppliers of auto parts such as Zhongce Rubber Group Co., Ltd., Haltec, and other complete vehicle manufacturers such as SAIC. It is a supporting supplier of many well-known automakers such as SAIC-GM, Volkswagen, BAIC, and GAC. It is also a supporting supplier of Alcoa, Volvo, etc., and faces the after-sales service market in Europe and America.

The acquired company, Westfalia Metal Hoses Group, under Heitkamp & Thumann Group (H&T), is specifically related with six companies: Westfalia Metallschlauchtechnik GmbH & Co. KG Germany Business Company (WSH), Westfalia Metal s.r.o. Czech Business Company (WCZ), Westfalia, Inc. American Business Company (WIW), Westfalia Shanghai Trading Company Ltd. (WSC), Westfalia Metal Components Shanghai Co., Ltd. (WSS) and Westfalia Grundstücks-GmbH & Co. KG (WGG).

WMHG is the world's leading supplier of complex components and the global market leader of airtight decoupling components for commercial vehicles, focusing on the production of exhaust pipe systems and decoupling components for commercial vehicles and other heavy transport vehicles. It also provides flexible metal hoses, airtight flexible damping components, elbows, insulation sleeves and exhaust pipe system assemblies for automobile exhaust systems worldwide, and is the only company with airtight solutions based on ribbon wound welded hoses.

Among them, WCZ, was registered and established in Brno, the Czech Republic in 2001. Fully controlled by Westfalia Metallslauchtechnik Verwaltungs-GmbH (WSV), an affiliated enterprise of Heitkamp & Thumann KG (H&T KG), it has a relatively perfect capability of assembly and manufacturing. Apart from the manufacturing of Strip Wound Hose (SWH), it undertakes the assembly of Gastight Hose (GTH) products, the production of metal hose end fittings, elbows and thermal insulation fittings.

2. Acquisition Case Profile

Acquirers: Hamaton and its wholly-owned subsidiaries CORE Mainstream Luxemburg S.A.R.L. (CORE Luxemburg) and CORE Mainstream Germany GmbH (CORE Germany).

Acquired party: H&T Group, specifically including H&T KG and its affiliated enterprises WSV and WGG.

Acquisition target: WMHG-related equity assets and non-equity assets, specifically involving WSH, WCZ, WIW, WSC, WSS and WGG. The details of transaction list are shown in Table 1-1.

Table 1-1   Trading List of Equity Assets and Non-Equity Assets

Equity assets

SN	Acquired party	Acquisition target	Acquired party Share holding ratio	Acquirer	Final purchase price (Euro)
1	H&T KG	WSH (Germany)	Limited partner's equity	CORE Germany	19,226,052
2	WSV	WCZ (the Czech Republic)	100%	CORE Germany	17,257,217
3	WSV	WIW (USA)	100%	CORE Germany	2,435,246
4	WSV	WSC (Shanghai, China)	100%	Hamaton	2,602,000
5	WSV	WSS (Shanghai, China)	100%	Hamaton	7,017,000

Non-equity assets

SN	Acquired party	Acquisition target	Acquirer	Final purchase price (Euro)
6	WGG	The land located in Hilchenbach, Germany, and all rights, obligations, houses and appurtenances attached thereto. The land was originally used by WSH, covering an area of 32,666 square meters	CORE Luxemburg	3,874,668

(**Source:** According to the *2019 Continuous Supervision Opinions of BOC International Securities Co., Ltd. on the Purchase of Major Assets of Hamaton Automotive Technology Co., Ltd.*)

Note: WSH is a limited partnership, WSV is its general partner and H&T KG is its limited partner. When H&T KG transfers its 100% limited partner interest of WSH to the buyer, WSV cancels its general partner interest.

Transaction price: The final purchase price is EUR 52,412,183, of which the final purchase price of WCZ was EUR 17,257,217.

Payment method: By cash. By May 2020, all payments have been accomplished and WCZ has completed the acquisition in September 2019.

Changes in equity: This acquisition involved changes in the ownership structure. The ownership structure between the acquirer and the acquired after the acquisition is shown in Figure 1-4.

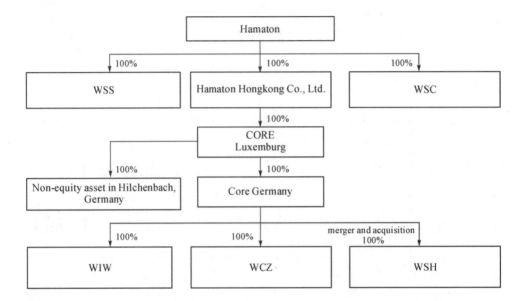

Figure 1-4   The Relationship between the Acquirer and the Acquired after the Acquisition

(**Source:** *Report on the Implementation of Major Asset Purchase of Hamaton Automotive Technology Co., Ltd.*)

3. Impact Analysis

The acquisition of WMHG by Hamaton not only constitutes a major asset restructuring for the acquirer, but also brings positive effects such as resource integration, international layout and brand superposition.

(1) Resource Integration Effect

It can generate synergy for Hamaton with WMHG in the key fields of commercial vehicle auto parts. Through the integration of R&D teams, marketing teams and sales channels, Hamaton can provide comprehensive auto parts products and services to commercial vehicle manufacturers in a better method.

(2) International Layout Effect

Through this acquisition, Hamaton can quickly complete its international layout with its R&D, production and sales bases in the United States, European countries and China, covering all major markets across the globe. It can also further understand the overseas market environment, business environment and legal environment, and enrich its management experience as a multinational enterprise.

(3) Brand Superposition Effect

By brand virtue of WMHG, Hamaton can actively start the layout of international market and promote the multi-brand strategy. At the same time, WMHG can further explore the domestic market by the domestic popularity and market status of Hamaton, so as to enhance the comprehensive competitiveness of Hamaton.

III. People-to-People Exchanges

1. The Education Cooperation Platform Is Actively Built and the Development Space Is Constantly Expanding

In 2019, the theme of China-CEEC cooperation was "the Year of Education and Youth Exchange". At the 8th Summit of China and Central and Eastern European Countries, the *Dubrovnik Guidelines for Cooperation between China and Central and Eastern European Countries* was also released, which clarified five aspects of cooperation in education, youth and sports. Guided by the spirit of the new outline, Zhejiang has continuously expanded cooperation with Central and Eastern European Countries in the field of education, explored new modes of educational cooperation, and effectively promoted the scope and elevated the level of educational cooperation between Zhejiang and the Czech Republic.

In February, the Ministry of Education and Ningbo Municipal Government signed the *Memorandum of International Cooperation on Promoting the Education of the Belt and Road Initiative*, focusing on supporting Ningbo to carry out the international cooperation experiment of the Belt and Road education, holding the dialogue of education policy between China and Central and Eastern European Countries, strengthening foreign aid training for vocational education as well as running schools abroad. In May, during the visit of Che Jun, the then secretary of Zhejiang Provincial Party Committee to the Czech Republic, China Jiliang University and University of Financial and Administration in Prague jointly established Zhejiang-Czech Humanities Exchange Center and Central and Eastern Europe Research Institute. Zhejiang Financial College signed a cooperation agreement with the Belt and Road Initiative Czech Station to explore the co-construction of the Silk Road College. It also signed a memorandum of AV21 strategic research project on

"Global Conflict and Local Interaction" with the Global Research Center of Czech Academy of Sciences.

Meanwhile, the Belt and Road Initiative Language College of Zhejiang Wanli University was established, and the first order class in Czech completed the program. From July to August, the 4th Zhejiang University Graduate International Workshop Project was held in Mendel University, the Czech Republic, involving academic lectures by top Czech professors, visits to important international organizations, practical research activities in four countries of Central and Eastern Europe, etc. In October, the opening ceremony of the 6th China (Ningbo)-CEEC Educational Cooperation Conference and the Belt and Road Countries Education Cooperation Summit was held in Ningbo. Seven educational and cultural centers were unveiled and seven educational cooperation agreements were signed, among which Ningbo Dongqian Lake Tourism School signed a pairing agreement with Czech Gemegis International Tourism School.

In addition, Zhejiang Ocean University and Prague University of Life Sciences signed a memorandum of cooperation in the fields of biotechnology, environmental technology and food processing technology. Ningbo College of Health Sciences signed a cooperation agreement with Prague College of Medical Nursing and reached consensuses on cooperation in medical education and health care. In Zhejiang Financial College, the only Czech Pavilion established by the college in China, actively serves related universities, enterprises and associations, receiving nearly 6,000 visitors every year.

2. Tourism Boom Cooled Down, and the Speed of Growth Turned from Rising to Falling

In recent years, the number of Chinese tourists to the Czech Republic has continued to grow at a high level, yet in 2019 the growth rate turned from increasing to decreasing with a slight decline. According to the data of the Czech Bureau of Statistics, China has been the fourth largest source country of foreign tourists to the Czech Republic for two consecutive years. In 2019, 612,000 Chinese tourists traveled to the Czech Republic, representing a year-on-year decline of 1%. Among them, the decrease of Chinese tourists in the third quarter accounted largely for the annual decline, in certain degree related to the high base of the early stage as well as other factors.

Although Sino-Czech tourism boom slightly cooled down to some extent, the rich and attractive tourism resources of the Czech Republic are in line with the upgrading of tourism consumption in Zhejiang. And the tourism cooperation and interaction between Zhejiang and the Czech Republic are still frequent. In May, the Zhejiang (Ningbo)-Czech Seminar on Economic and Technological Cooperation hosted by the Zhejiang Provincial Government and undertaken by the Ningbo Municipal Government was held in Prague. The Ningbo Municipal Bureau of Culture, Radio, Television and Tourism signed a cultural tourism cooperation project with the Czech side to further develop the two-way tourism market.

In June, the first China-Central and Eastern European Countries Expo was launched in Ningbo, in which the Czech Republic, Poland, Slovakia, Hungary and other countries actively promoted its tourism with their own characteristics at the special matchmaking meeting for tourism of the Central and Eastern Europe while the Czech Republic, as the leading country, shared a series of unique tourism routes. Meanwhile, China Travel Service Zhejiang Group Co., Ltd. signed a million-dollar purchase order with Wings Travel, mainly in responsible for docking Czech tourism resources. The pandemic in 2020 has imposed unprecedented impact on international tourism. With the pandemic situation taking a favorable turn, the tourism cooperation between Zhejiang and the Czech Republic will gradually resume, but the recovery period will be longer.

3. Cultural Exchanges Yield Rich Diversity, Building a Bridge Connecting People on Both Sides

The year of 2019 coincided with the 70th anniversary of the establishment of diplomatic relations between China and the Czech Republic. The cultural and artistic exchange activities between the two sides are rich and colorful. Zhejiang also contributes to the promotion of cultural exchange and integration between the two sides. In January, the Chen Meilan New Drama Creation Team of Zhejiang Wu Theater visited the Czech Republic, giving five performances in three cities, namely Prague, Ostrava and Olomz. With the theme of "Happy Spring Festival, Beautiful Zhejiang", the performance displayed classic Wu Opera, Zhejiang folk customs, traditional Chinese culture and Czech ballads by arranging classic programs such as "The Heavenly Maids Scatter Blossoms", "Jiangnan Silk and Bamboo Ensemble", "Nine Festival Dragons", "Rap: Facial Make-up of Beijing Opera", "Opera Martial Arts" and "Czech Folk Songs Ensemble". It has deepened Czech people's understanding of the traditional culture of Zhejiang Province, and narrowed the distance between them.

In May 2019, a series of European cultural activities of Zhejiang Province were launched in the Czech Republic. The exhibition "Silk, Tea and Porcelain, Cross-cultural Dialogue on the Silk Road" was held in Pilsen Region. The exhibition was divided into five sections: source, road, art, utensil and cultural fusion. The evolution history and artistic changes of silk, tea and porcelain in Zhejiang over thousands of years was introduced in detail via the display of fine products of Zhejiang silk, tea and porcelain, the dissemination of cultural symbols as well as the exchange and interaction on the spot. It comprehensively displayed the history and cultural connotation of "silk, tea and porcelain" from the aspects of historical origin of silk and tea, the exchange between the east and the west, art inheritance and development.

In the meantime, educational and cultural exchange performances were held by Hangzhou Wenlan Middle School and Czech Otna Middle School at the ZIBA Building of the former Czech National Bank, the key cultural relics protection units in Prague. In August,

16

Development Report on Zhejiang-Czech Economic and Trade
Cooperation under the Framework of the Belt and Road Initiative (2020)

the opening ceremony of the Prague special exhibition of "Centenary of Xiling Engravers' Society" and the exchange activities of artistic creation, co-hosted by the Belt and RoadCzech Station and Xiling Seal Engravers Society were held in Zhejiang Silk Road Center. Adopting an integrated display method combining on-the-spot creation and art display, the special exhibition has showcased the special charm of Chinese art. On the one hand, the artists of Xiling Seal Engravers Society have demonstrated Chinese traditional literati temperament and oriental artistic beauty of knives carving and art via the art of seal cutting, painting and calligraphy, an inspiring on-spot artistic exchange. On the other hand, 48 original seals of "People's Olympics" and 70 paintings and calligraphy works created by artists from Xiling Seal Engravers Society were displayed in the form of on-the-spot exhibition, an artistic feast, thus deepening people's understanding of Chinese artistic craftsmanship.

IV. Joint-efforts-to-fight-against-pandemic Analysis

1. The Progress of the Czech Republic's Fight against COVID-19

Since the first COVID-19 confirmed case was discovered on March 1, 2020, the Czech Republic has implemented strict epidemic prevention and control measures in a timely manner. It was one of the first countries in the European Union to declare a state of emergency, close its borders and force people to wear masks in public. With the rapid response and targeted measures, the Czech Republic has become the first country to announce deregulation from the unfavorable situation of the most confirmed cases in the early stage of the outbreak in Central and Eastern Europe, showing extremely high efficiency in epidemic prevention and control. From the occurrence of confirmed cases on March 1 to the deregulation node on May 25, the progress of the Czech Republic's fight against COVID-19 could be roughly divided into three stages.

(1) First Stage: The Epidemic Spreading Period (March 1 to March 21)

The Czech Republic announced three COVID-19 confirmed cases for the first time on March 1, and half a month later it became the country with the most confirmed cases among the 17 countries in the Central and Eastern Europe. As shown in Figure 1-5, from March 1 to March 21, more than 1,000 COVID-19 cases in total were diagnosed in the Czech Republic, and the cumulative positive rate was rising continuously, reaching a maximum of 6.6% on March 21. From the source of infection, the Czech epidemic originated from northern Italy, where the epidemic saw its most serious condition in Europe at that time. According to the data from the Czech Ministry of Health, there were about 16,500 Czechs in Italy at the beginning of March, most of whom were vacationers. With the continuous development of the epidemic, the sources of infection tended to be diversified, and some cases of infection were related to Austria, Germany, the United States and Spain. In terms of regional distribution, Prague was infected most seriously, followed by Central Bohemia, Olomouc Jordan Mutch, Usti and Zlin.

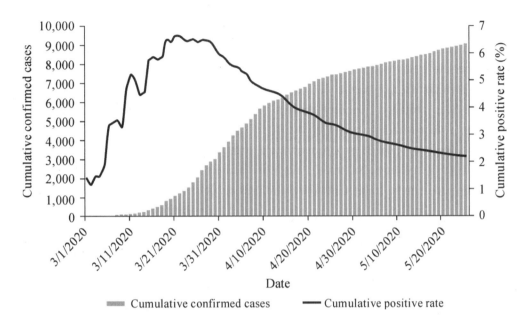

Figure 1-5   Cumulative COVID-19 Confirmed Cases in the Czech Republic from March 1 to May 25, 2020

(**Source:** Czech Ministry of Health)

Note: Cumulative positive rate refers to the proportion of cumulative positive cases (confirmed cases) to the total number of cumulative tests.

In the face of the COVID-19 epidemic, the Czech government quickly took action, intensively introducing a series of strict control measures which were continuously upgraded (as shown in Table 1-2).

1) In terms of national management, the World Health Organization (WHO) identified the novel coronavirus as a global pandemic. On March 12, the Czech government declared a 30-day state of emergency in which the government collectively managed the country in times of crisis and postponed it twice until May 17. State of emergency is a crisis measure taken by the Czech government. In severe cases, COVID-19 would seriously endanger people's lives, health and property safety, and even national order and security.

2) In terms of entry and exit and flow of people, it was announced on March 2 that the Czech government suspended the flights to and from R.O. Korea and northern Italian cities; on March 7, it announced the suspension of issuing visas to Iranian citizens, upgraded to stop issuing all visas on March 14; on March 9, random temperature measurement

18

Development Report on Zhejiang-Czech Economic and Trade
Cooperation under the Framework of the Belt and Road Initiative (2020)

inspections were carried out at 10 border crossings in the Czech Republic. At the same time, troops were mobilized to the borders with Germany and Austria to strictly enforce the control. The borders with Poland and Slovakia were also controlled by the two countries. On March 10, it was decided to ban civil servants from international travel and business trips, and special matters should be approved by ministers. On March 16, the ban on the free movement of persons came into effect, which prohibited the free movement of natural persons in the Czech Republic. At the same time, all foreigners were prohibited from entering the Czech Republic and all Czech people were prohibited from leaving the country. This has been the most stringent prevention and control measure taken by the Czech government since March 1.

3) In terms of inspection and quarantine, a group of laboratories were set up to test and evaluate the collected samples. And home sampling measures were implemented to encourage people to be isolated at home, and medical staff were sent to collect samples for inspection by telephone or e-mail, so as to reduce the possibility of virus transmission. The 14-day compulsory quarantine rule was implemented for all returnees from Italy from March 7, and extended to returnees from 15 high-risk countries including China on March 13.

4) In terms of epidemic prevention materials, export, sales price and mask wearing were strictly controlled. From March 4, it was forbidden to export FFP3 masks, and new regulations on drug circulation were introduced to forbid supplying all authorized medicinal products originally planned to be sold in the Czech market to European Union (EU) countries, or exported to other countries outside the EU. The Czech Ministry of Finance announced the control of mask prices. The limited price of masks produced in EU countries is CZK 175 per piece (excluding VAT, the same below), and CZK 350 per piece in non-EU countries. On March 19, the compulsory wearing of masks or other respiratory protective equipment in public places was implemented, and the Czech government also approved the allocation of CZK 500 million from the government budget reserve to the Ministry of Health to guarantee the purchase of necessary medical protective equipment.

5) In terms of business premises and group activities, schools, shops, restaurants, public venues, etc. were shut down, and the number of people in various assembly activities was limited. From March 11, primary schools, middle schools, colleges and universities and higher education institutions all over the country were closed, involving about 1.7 million students. With the support of the Ministry of Education, Czech Television has started a "TV class" for students since March 16 to alleviate the problem of school suspension for children and their parents, which was tentatively scheduled to run for one month. There were not only low-grade courses, but also high-grade courses such as physics, geography and history. The Czech government also forced full-time students in colleges and universities to study social and humanitarian work, social law, social pedagogy, social nursing, social pathology, etc., and feel obligated to provide assistance if necessary. From

March 11, all gathering activities with more than 100 people were banned, and all castles, museums, libraries, art galleries were closed. Starting from March 13, the government further tightened these measures, reducing the maximum number of participants in any activity to 30, prohibiting the public from entering sports fields, fitness centers, swimming pools, social clubs, etc., and closing all restaurants, bars, casinos, stall markets, shopping centers, beauty shops, barber shops and other service providers except grocery stores, pharmacies, gas stations, pet shops and some other stores.

Table 1-2 Important Chronicle of Czech's Fight against COVID-19
from March 1 to May 25, 2020

Time	Chronicle of the fight against COVID-19
March 1	● The Czech Republic announced three COVID-19 confirmed cases for the first time
March 2	● Flights between the Czech Republic and R. O. Korea / northern Italian cities were suspended
March 4	● It was prohibited to export FFP3 masks which could only be sold to health and social institutions, public health departments, comprehensive rescue systems and other state administrative agencies under the regulations—the ban was lifted one month later
March 7	● The 14-day compulsory quarantine rule was implemented for all returnees from Italy, and those who violated the regulations would face a fine of up to CZK 3 million
March 9	● Random temperature measurement inspections on travelers were carried out at 10 border crossings in the Czech Republic; at the same time, troops were mobilized to the borders with Germany and Austria to strictly enforce the control (The borders with Poland and Slovakia were also controlled by these two countries)
March 10	● Civil servants were banned from international travel and business trips, and special matters should be approved by ministers ● Outsiders were prohibited from visiting inpatient departments and nursing homes
March 11	● All primary and secondary schools (except kindergartens), colleges and universities and higher education institutions in the Czech Republic were closed ● All cultural and sports social activities involving more than 100 people were prohibited, including gathering activities such as literature and art, sports, religion, celebrations, fairs, etc.—this prohibition was not applicable to funerals and meetings of legislation, public administration and court trials ● All castles, museums, libraries, art galleries were closed
March 12	● The Czech government declared a 30-day state of emergency from 14:00 on that day, which was valid from March 12 to April 11

20

Development Report on Zhejiang-Czech Economic and Trade
Cooperation under the Framework of the Belt and Road Initiative (2020)

Continued

March 13	● The 14-day compulsory quarantine for returnees from abroad was applicable to 15 selected high epidemic risk countries, including China, R.O. Korea, Iran, Italy, Spain, Austria, Germany, Switzerland, Sweden, Netherlands, Belgium, Britain, Norway, Denmark and France ● All gathering activities with more than 30 people were prohibited ● The public were prohibited from entering sports fields, fitness centers, swimming pools, social clubs, etc.
March 14	● All visas were stopped issuing ● The implementation of the ban on passenger transport of more than 9 people in the Czech Republic were applicable to all cross-border railway and bus transport ● All restaurants, bars, casinos, stall markets, shopping centers, beauty shops, barber shops and other service providers were closed except grocery stores, pharmacies, gas stations, pet shops and some other stores
March 15	● The Czech government issued a ban on the free movement of people, which came into effect from 00: 00 on March 16 to 06:00 on March 24: Free movement of people was prohibited in the Czech Republic, except for commuting and purchasing necessary daily necessities; all foreigners were prohibited from entering the Czech Republic, while all Czechs were prohibited from leaving the country—this ban was not applicable to truck drivers, train workers, aircraft workers and workers from neighboring countries living within 100 km of the Czech border with Austria and Germany (approval required)
March 18	● Imposed a curfew
March 19	● The compulsory wearing of masks or other respiratory protective equipment in public places was implemented, and the violator would face a fine of up to CZK 10,000
March 28	● The intelligent quarantine system of COVID-19 was started, tested in South Moravia, North Moravia and Prague successively, and popularized and implemented nationwide on April 13
March 30	● The ban on the free movement of people was extended until April 11 ● The restrictions on hotels and hostels were loosened up, and they were allowed to receive accommodation customers for work or business needs
April 2	● The 14-day compulsory quarantine was imposed on all people returning to the Czech Republic, with the exception of cross-border workers, medical personnel, social rescue service personnel, diplomats and blood transport personnel
April 3	● The border control between the Czech Republic and Germany/Austria was extended to April 24th
April 9	● The state of emergency was extended to April 30

Continued

April 14	• The limited restrictions on entry and exit were implemented, and people were allowed to leave the Czech Republic for "necessary purposes", such as business trips, medical treatment or visiting relatives, but they must observe the 14-day self-quarantine at home after returning to the homeland • The Czech government announced a deregulation plan, gradually relaxing or cancelling some epidemic prevention and control measures in five stages from April 20 to June 8, and might make adjustments at any time according to the epidemic situation: In the first stage, starting from April 20, farmer's markets, handicraft shops, car dealerships, outdoor training grounds for professional athletes (no audience allowed) would be opened, and small weddings with less than 10 people could also be held; in the second stage, starting from April 27, shops within 200 square meters were allowed to operate, but shops in large shopping centers (more than 5,000 square meters) were still not allowed to operate; in the third stage, starting from May 11, shops within 1,000 square meters, driving schools and the fitness areas in gyms (except dressing rooms and bathing facilities) would be opened; in the fourth stage, starting from May 25, the outdoor areas of cafes, bars and restaurants were allowed to operate, so were barbershops, beauty salons, massage shops, museums and art galleries; in the fifth stage, starting from June 8, cafes, bars, restaurants, hotels, taxis, large shopping malls over 5,000 square meters, theaters, castles and other places or services could be resumed, and cultural, sports or commercial activities with less than 50 people were also allowed
April 20	• The Czech government decided that administrative departments (such as state, municipal or regional offices) could be fully operational from April 20
April 23	• The Czech government speeded up the deregulation plan by 14 days, adjusted from "five stages" to "four stages", that is, the deregulation plan would be implemented in four stages from April 20 to May 25 • According to the gradual opening-up plan of the Czech government, the schedule for students to return to school was determined (for example, all students in Czech universities could return to school on April 27, and the first stage of Czech primary school began on May 25); the Ministry of Education also formulated corresponding epidemic prevention manuals for students returning to school
April 24	• The ban on free movement of people and foreign travel was canceled, and their people were allowed to leave the country, however, if they returned to the Czech Republic, they had to present a negative report of COVID-19 test or finish the 14-day self-isolation

Continued

April 24	● The border control between the Czech Republic and Germany/Austria was extended to May 14 ● The limited number of peers in public places increased from 2 to 10
April 27	● Shopping malls within 2,500 square meters were allowed to operate, while shops in shopping centers were still not allowed ● Outdoor areas such as zoos and fitness centers also would be opened
April 28	● The state of emergency was extended to May 17
May 1	● Appropriate relaxation of the "Mask-wearing Order"
May 11	● All shopping centers, barber shops, beauty salons, outdoor gardens of restaurants, museums, art galleries, theaters, cinemas, concert halls were allowed to resume operation, and activities for up to 100 people were allowed to hold ● Twenty-seven Czech embassies and consulates abroad resumed visa processing, including China—Chengdu, China—Beijing and China—Shanghai ● Resumed cross-border railway and bus operations
May 18	● The state of emergency officially ended
May 25	● The government approved people to go out without wearing a mask, referring to the termination of the mandatory requirement on wearing a mask in outdoor public places ● Restaurants, cafes, bars, castles, swimming pools were reopened, and activities for up to 300 people were allowed

(**Source:** It was continuously tracked and collated according to the information released by Czech government departments.)

(2) Second Stage: The Epidemic Outbreak Period (March 22 to April 9)

In the second stage, the COVID-19 confirmed cases in the Czech Republic increased rapidly and entered the peak period of outbreak, having been the country with the most confirmed cases among the 17 countries in Central and Eastern Europe. As shown in Figures 1-5 and 1-6, the average number of COVID-19 confirmed cases in the Czech Republic was about 240 per day from March 22 to April 9, more than 4 times of the average number of confirmed cases in the first stage (50 cases), reaching the highest number (377 cases) on March 27. There were a total of 5,591 COVID-19 confirmed cases, among which it exceeded 2,000 on March 26, 3,000 on March 30, 4,000 on April 3, and 5,000 on April 7, each spanning 4 days, much faster than the first-stage growth rate (An exceedance of 1,000 cases with a span of 20 days). As to the source of infection, most of the infections in the second stage originated domestically, while most of the foreign infections originated from Austria, followed by Italy. According to the regional distribution, Prague was still the most seriously infected area, followed by Central Bohemia, Moravia-Silesia Olomouc Jordan Mutch and South Moravia. It was worth noting that the positive rate index has improved significantly, with the daily positive rate dropping from 6.4% on March 22 to 3.1% on April 9, and the cumulative positive rate dropping from 6.6% on March 22 to 4.7% on April 9. Although the two positive rate indexes still remained at a relatively high level, the downward trend showed that the Czech epidemic was gradually being contained.

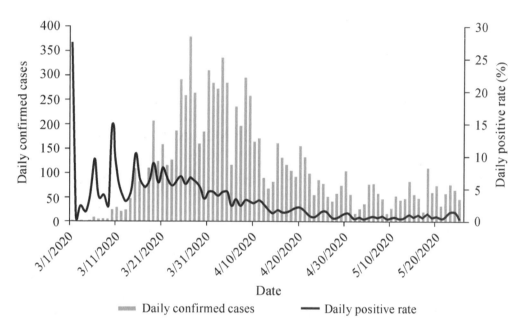

Figure 1-6　Daily COVID-19 Confirmed Cases in the Czech Republic from March 1 to May 25, 2020

(**Source:** Czech Ministry of Health)

Note: Daily positive rate refers to the proportion of daily positive cases (confirmed cases) to the total number of cumulative tests.

At this stage, the Czech government continued to introduce a number of control measures in national management, entry and exit, flow of people, inspection and quarantine. In terms of national management, on April 9, the Czech House of Representatives approved the extension of the state of emergency to April 30 (originally scheduled for April 11). In terms of entry and exit and flow of people, on March 30, the Czech government announced that the restrictions on the free movement of people would be extended to April 11; on April 3, the Czech government decided to extend the land and air border control with Germany and Austria until April 24. At the same time, since Poland and Slovakia had implemented border control over the Czech Republic, they would not repeat the control. To support border control initiatives, the Czech government allocated CZK 18.1 million from the budget

24

Development Report on Zhejiang-Czech Economic and Trade
Cooperation under the Framework of the Belt and Road Initiative (2020)

reserve to the Ministry of Interior. In terms of inspection and quarantine, the Czech government started the intelligent quarantine system on March 28, firstly completing the test in South Moravia and gradually spreading it to the whole country. Co-developed by the Czech government and the military, the system can investigate the modes and channels of COVID-19 infection through random tests, and quickly track and identify the close contacts of confirmed patients. On April 2, the 14-day compulsory quarantine rule was implemented for all people returning to the Czech Republic, which previously was only applicable to people returning from high-risk areas. According to the survey conducted by the Czech's authoritative survey agency STEM at the end of March, most Czechs highly praised the prevention and control measures taken by the Czech government in response to the COVID-19 epidemic crisis.

(3) Third Stage: The Epidemic Outbreak Period (March 22 to April 9)

In the third stage, the situation of epidemic prevention and control in the Czech Republic was improved, and the spread of the virus was curbed to some extent. Among the 17 countries in Central and Eastern Europe, the cumulative number of COVID-19 confirmed cases in the Czech Republic was surpassed by Poland on April 10, and then successively overtaken by Romania and Serbia, the Czech Republic falling back to the fourth place from the country with the most confirmed cases originally. As shown in Figures 1-5 and 1-6, from April 10 to May 25, the average number of COVID-19 confirmed cases in the Czech Republic was about 75 per day, less than one third of the average number of confirmed cases every day in the second stage. There were a total of 9,025 COVID-19 confirmed cases, among which it exceeded 6,000 cases on April 12, 7,000 cases on April 21, 8,000 cases on May 7 and 9,000 cases on May 25, and the time span of exceeding 1,000 cases was continuously lengthened. At the same time, the positive rate index was further improved, and the average daily positive rate was 1.2%, lower than 6.7% in the first stage and 4.8% in the second stage, at a relatively low level. The cumulative positive rate decreased continuously from 4.7% on April 10 to 2.2% on May 25. All the above indicators showed that the spreading speed of the Czech epidemic slowed down, and the previous prevention and control measures achieved phased results.

As the situation improved, the Czech government gradually began deregulation, lifted the restrictive epidemic prevention measures, and promoted the work and production resumption in an orderly manner. In terms of the national management, on April 28, the Czech House of Representatives approved the extension of the national emergency to May 17 (originally scheduled for April 30), that is, the Czech national emergency officially ended on May 18. In terms of entry and exit and flow of people, the Czech Republic began to implement the limited relaxation program on entry and exit on April 14, and lifted the ban on free movement of people and foreign travel on April 24. From May 11, some Czech embassies and consulates abroad resumed visa processing. In terms of mask protection, the

Czech government decided to appropriately relax the "Mask-wearing Order" from May 1, and on May 25 further approved that people can go out without wearing masks, that is, to end the mandatory requirement of wearing masks in outdoor public places. In terms of business premises and group activities, the Czech government announced a deregulation plan, gradually relaxing or canceling some epidemic prevention and control measures in five stages from April 20 to June 8, and later accelerating the pace of deregulation, from "five stages" to "four stages", that is, the deregulation plan was implemented in four stages from April 20 to May 25. In addition, in order to alleviate the impact of special measures on Czech enterprises and families during the epidemic, the Czech government took some compensation measures, including allowing postponement of tax reports and exemption of late payment fees, allowing deferred installment payments, allowing individual business households not to pay social insurance advance payments from March to August, reducing some hospital debts, suspending electronic sales registration (EET), providing subsidies for individual business households, nursing staff or temporary workers, paying wages and providing interest-free loans, credit guarantees, fiscal subsidies and export credit guarantees for enterprises, amending the Bankruptcy Law, and supporting cultural industries and the cut in interest rates of Czech Central Bank (CNB) with special funds.

After the implementation of easing measures in the Czech Republic, the COVID-19 confirmed cases did not increase sharply, still keeping 50 new cases per day on average until mid-June. However, it was not excluded that local epidemic prevention measures would be activated again if regional and clustered infections emerged.

2. Joint Fight against Pandemic between China (Zhejiang) and the Czech Republic

During the period of fighting against the epidemic in Czech, China helped and shared its experience in a timely manner, and Zhejiang also took the initiative. China (Zhejiang) and the Czech Republic have further enhanced friendship and cooperation in the joint fight against the pandemic.

At the national level, when China was at a critical time in the fight against the epidemic, the Czech Republic donated epidemic prevention materials to China. At the beginning of the epidemic outbreak in the Czech Republic, China fully assisted in solving difficulties and actively promoted bilateral anti-epidemic cooperation through various means such as the supply of epidemic prevention materials and the sharing of information and experience. In early March, Vratislav Mynář, Special Envoy of President of the Czech Republic and Head of the Presidential Office of the Czech Republic, donated 5 tons of epidemic prevention materials during his visit to China. Later, considering the increasingly serious epidemic situation in the Czech Republic and the practical difficulties of serious shortage of epidemic prevention materials, China decided to keep 4 tons of the donated materials in the Czech Republic to support its fight against epidemic. At the same time, China urgently coordinated with the Ministry of Foreign Affairs, the Ministry of Commerce, customs, civil aviation, banks and other departments and institutions, and opened up the "Air Freight Transport Corridor" and "Green Channel for Financial Services" to facilitate and support the Czech Republic's procurement of epidemic prevention materials in China, becoming the first country to provide the Czech Republic with epidemic prevention supplies. The Czech government also actively responded to the epidemic through global procurement, but most materials came from China. According to the data from the Chinese Embassy in the Czech Republic and Eastern Airlines, from March 20 to May 3, there were a total of 51 special government chartered flights for the Czech epidemic prevention, delivering about 2,000 tons, nearly CZK 4 billion, including masks, protective masks, respirators, protective clothing and test kits. It turned out that thanks to China's support, the shortage of epidemic prevention materials in the Czech Republic was greatly alleviated. In addition, China also held many video conferences to exchange information on anti-epidemic, share experience in prevention and control, and exchange diagnosis and treatment programs. For example, on March 13, China held a video conference with 17 countries in Central and Eastern Europe on COVID-19 prevention and control, sharing prevention and control experience with public health experts from other countries, including the Czech Republic, for reference in epidemic prevention practice.

At the provincial level, with the spread of the epidemic in the Czech Republic, all sectors of society in Zhejiang raced against the clock to assist it, government agencies, non-governmental organizations, enterprises and overseas Chinese actively donating epidemic prevention materials to help the Czech Republic fight against the epidemic. With the support from government agencies, the United Front Department of the Zhejiang Provincial Committee and the Zhejiang Federation of Returned Overseas Chinese jointly donated 50,000 masks, which were distributed free of charge to overseas Chinese in the Czech Council by the Promotion of Peaceful National Reunification of China and Qingtian Association of the Czech Republic; the United Front Work Department of Ningbo Municipal Committee and the Municipal Federation of Returned Overseas Chinese jointly donated 12,000 masks and entrusted the Eastern and Central Europe Trade Union to distribute them; the United Front Work Department of Qingtian County Committee donated Chinese medicine anti-epidemic granules, distributed by the Czech-Central Europe Chamber of Commerce and Industry. In terms of the support from non-governmental organizations, the Czech Chinese Volunteer League for Anti-epidemic was established to carry out emergency services such as food and medicine delivery, distribution of materials, medical consultation and translation. Zhejiang Eternal Love Foundation and Wenzhou Blazing Youth Community donated protective articles, some to hospitals in Budějovice, the Czech Republic, and some to Chinese students, overseas Chinese and some social service organizations. In terms of hospital and enterprise support, Zhejiang Provincial Hospital of Chinese Medicine, Zhejiang Jolly Pharmaceutical Co., Ltd., Huadong Medicine Co., Ltd. and Zhejiang Shouxiangu

Pharmaceutical Co., Ltd. donated a batch of anti-epidemic and preventive Chinese medicines; Lishui Central Hospital opened the channel "Overseas Chinese Medical Service Express Train", arranging experts to provide online medical services for them; Dahua, a Zhejiang enterprise in the Czech Republic, donated infrared detection equipment to nursing homes in Usti. In early April, the Czech Foreign Ministry said Zhejiang had donated 100,000 masks, 20,000 respirators and 2,000 protective suits to the Central Army Hospital in Prague. Wenzhou and Qingtian, Lishui in Zhejiang are well-known hometowns of overseas Chinese who mainly live in Europe. A large part of Czech overseas Chinese come from Zhejiang, most from Wenzhou and Qingtian, Lishui. According to the statistics of Zhejiang Federation of Returned Overseas Chinese, more than 90% of the Czech overseas Chinese come from Wenzhou and Qingtian, Lishui, so this time Wenzhou and Qingtian, Lishui were especially active in supporting the Czech Republic in this epidemic .

China (Zhejiang)-Czech joint fight against the epidemic brought China (Zhejiang)-Czech relations closer and injected new energy into the friendship between the two sides. It is undeniable that there were various disharmonious factors during this period, from official voices and media channels, mainly about the criticism on the government for purchasing Chinese epidemic prevention materials at high prices, questioning of the quality of Chinese medical materials, Chinese businessmen's hoarding, etc. For example, in the process of aiding Europe, a batch of masks donated to European overseas Chinese by Qingtian, Zhejiang were requisitioned by the Czech local government, and the Czech media reported that Chinese businessmen made profits by hoarding. For any negative comments, the Czech President Milos Zeman, Prime Minister Andrej Babiš and the responsible person for epidemic prevention work directly retorted to or clarified the statement, and spoke highly of China's anti-pandemic effectiveness, thanking China for providing epidemic prevention materials to the Czech Republic in an emergency.

3. Suggestions on Promoting Zhejiang-Czech Economic and Trade Cooperation in Post-epidemic Period

For the economic recovery in the post-epidemic period, China and the Czech Republic further need the spirit of helping each other, deepening bilateral relations in practical cooperation. It is entirely possible for Zhejiang to shoulder this heavy burden, actively play the role of Zhejiang enterprises, overseas Chinese and open platform, and undertake the mission of "Important Window" to promote Zhejiang-Czech cooperation.

(1) Zhejiang Enterprises in the Czech Republic—the Important Carrier of Zhejiang-Czech Cooperation

Zhejiang enterprises, such as Wanxiang, Huajie, XZB, Dahua, Sunrise and CHINT, have invested and operated in the Czech Republic. Most of them base in the Czech Republic and radiate to Europe, forming a number of benchmark projects and achieving good results.

During the epidemic period, Zhejiang enterprises in the Czech Republic also faced difficulties in project implementation or operation in such a special period. As the epidemic situation in the Czech Republic improved day by day, these enterprises gradually returned to normal work and daily life. In the post-epidemic period, Zhejiang's key investment projects in the Czech Republic have entered a critical period of capital increase and production expansion, so it is urgent to implement detailed project tracking, accurately serve construction progress, and effectively solve difficulties in time for the enterprises in the Czech Republic. At the same time, the emerging investment fields are also facing a great opportunity period, focusing on the production and operation status of Czech enterprises in advantageous characteristic industries such as "automobile and parts", "nanotechnology", "biomedicine", "medical equipment" and "optical instruments", strengthening Zhejiang-Czech scientific and technological cooperation.

(2) Overseas Chinese from Zhejiang Province—the Important Force in Zhejiang-Czech Cooperation

"We will maintain extensive contact with overseas Chinese nationals, returned Chinese and their relatives and unite them so that they can join our endeavors to revitalize the Chinese nation" is a major strategic thinking established at the 19th National Congress of the Communist Party of China, and also an inevitable choice for China to start its reform and opening up in the new era. As the pioneer of reform and opening-up, Zhejiang people are brave in pioneering, venturing and fighting, forming a unique group of overseas Chinese from Zhejiang all over the world, which is a model of "jumping out of Zhejiang to develop Zhejiang". Chinese and overseas Chinese from Zhejiang form an important economic force in the "17+1 Cooperation" in Central and Eastern Europe, and an indispensable active factor in Zhejiang-Czech cooperation, which not only provides important intellectual support, but also plays a role as a bridge. The first generation of Zhejiang-born overseas Chinese in Czech has accumulated rich Chinese business network resources and strong capital foundation. With the upgrading of the knowledge level of the second and third generations, the new generation of overseas Chinese in Czech has a strong desire to innovate and start businesses in mainstream fields and return to participate in investment and trade, which meets the needs of Zhejiang-Czech development.

(3) Open Platform—the Important Support for Zhejiang-Czech Cooperation

From the perspective of national-level open platform, Zhejiang has the most active open platforms for institutional innovation in China, such as Zhoushan Free Trade Zone, Ningbo "17+1" Demonstration Zone for Economic and Trade Cooperation, 10 Cross-border E-commerce Comprehensive Pilot Reform Areas (basically achieving full coverage of the whole province except Zhoushan), Yiwu Pilot Comprehensive Reform of International Trade, and Yangtze River Delta Integration. From the exhibition layout, China CEEC Expo is the only national-level foreign-related institutional exhibition focusing on China-CEEC cooperation, and a number of import commodity exhibition and trading centers such as Yiwu China Imported Commodities Mall, Zhejiang Qingtian Imported Commodity City and Pinghu International Imported Commodity City have formed scale. From the perspective of the open platform in the Czech Republic, the Belt and Road Czech Station has become a provincial-level overseas economic and trade cooperation zone in Zhejiang. In the new historical position, the strategic layout of the above-mentioned series of open platforms will play an important role in the Zhejiang-Czech cooperation, and provide important support for the further economic recovery and integration of both sides in the post-epidemic period.

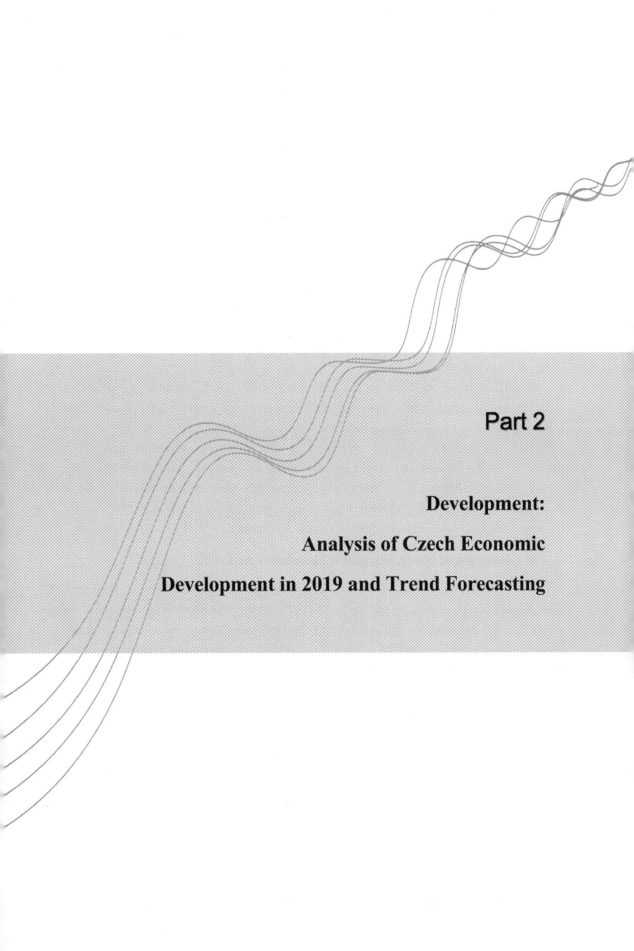

Part 2

Development:

Analysis of Czech Economic

Development in 2019 and Trend Forecasting

32

Development Report on Zhejiang-Czech Economic and Trade
Cooperation under the Framework of the Belt and Road Initiative (2020)

Introduction

◆ Overview of Czech Economic Development in 2019

In 2019, the Czech economy was in lower development level than expected, with the growth rate reaching the lowest in five years. In that year, the total GDP of the Czech Republic reached CZK 5,748.668 billion (equivalent to USD 250.661 billion), the per capita GDP reached USD 23,493.65, and the annual GDP actually increased by 2.3%, which was the lowest level in recent five years. Industry, especially manufacturing industry, contributed the most to the Czech GDP, especially automobile manufacturing, machinery and equipment, metal products and other industries.

In 2019, domestic demand was the main driver of the Czech economic growth, with a contribution rate as high as 98.1%, among which household consumption was still strong and had its own dynamic. In 2019, the import and export trade of Czech goods relatively declined compared with those in 2018, and the growth rate turned from positive to negative. More than 70% of goods trade was carried out within the EU, and the concentration of trade countries was high. Machinery and transportation equipment were the main trade categories in the Czech Republic, with high concentration of trade commodities. Inflation and fiscal deficit has been rising, and macroeconomic policies are under pressure.

◆ Forecast of Czech Economic Development Trend

In 2020, affected by the COVID-19 pandemic and various ban measures, the Czech economy will fall into recession, and its growth rate will drop sharply. It is estimated that the annual GDP would shrink by 8.2%. Under the background of continuous efforts of various economic stimulus policies and the low base in 2020, the economic growth rate of the Czech Republic will pick up in 2021, which is expected to increase by 3.5%, but it is still difficult to return to the pre-pandemic level, and the economic recovery process is slow.

The favorable factors for the Czech economic growth in 2020 mainly include a good foundation for economic recovery, strong support for investment and development, and favorable economic stimulus policies; unfavorable factors mainly include the weak and uncertain external demand, the sluggish domestic segmenting market and restricted labor mobility.

The Czech economy was in lower development level than expected, and the growth rate was the lowest in five years, with an increase of 2.3%. In 2020, affected by the COVID-19 pandemic and various ban measures, the economy will fall into recession, and the growth rate will drop sharply, which was expected to shrink by 8.2%. Domestic demand is still an important engine of Czech economic growth, among which household consumption is a major driver that could prop the investment development up. External demand is weak and full of uncertainty, and international trade and investment are weak. Market segments are facing the challenge of weakening both sides of supply and demand, and there are difficulties in staged development. The duration of the pandemic and the effectiveness of policy response are important variables. External risk factors such as the escalation of trade protectionism, the decline of Sino-US relations and the Brexit increase the difficulty coefficient, and the Czech economic recovery is likely to last for a long time.

I. Overview of Czech Economic Development in 2019

1. In 2019, the Czech Economy Grew Slower than Expected, and the Growth Rate Was the Lowest in Five Years

In 2019, the total GDP of the Czech Republic reached CZK 5,748.668 billion (equivalent to USD 250.661 billion at an annual average exchange rate of 2.2934, the same below), with an actual increase of 2.3%, which was lower than the full-year forecast of 2.5% by the Czech Ministry of Finance and 2.6% by the Czech National Bank, and decreased by 0.9%, compared with that in 2018, with the lowest increase in the past five years (as shown in Figure 2-1). In mid-2019, the population size was 10,669,300, and the annual per capita GDP reached USD 23,493.65, which was 2.3 times of China's per capita GDP and 1.5 times of Zhejiang's in the same year.

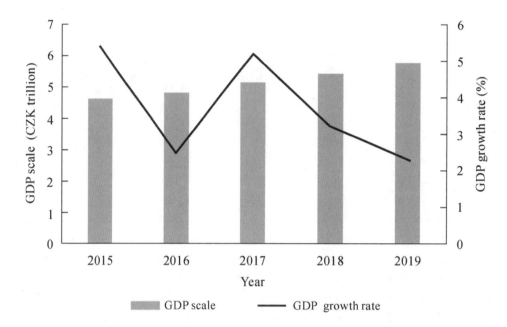

Figure 2-1   Czech GDP Scale and Its Growth Rate from 2015 to 2019

(**Source:** Czech Statistical Office)

Note: GDP scale is the price data of the current year, and the growth rate is the constant price data of 2015, the same below.

By quarters, the Czech GDP in the first quarter of 2019 had a year-on-year increase by 2.5%, the lowest growth rate in the past ten quarters. The actual growth rate of GDP in the second quarter further slowed down to 2.1%. In the third quarter, driven by the growth of household consumption and capital expenditure, GDP improved with the actual growth rate rebounding to 3.0% year-on-year. In the fourth quarter, GDP performance was weak, and the real growth rate dropped to 1.7% again, which was the lowest level of quarterly growth in recent five years. As an open economy, the economic performance of the Czech Republic is closely related to the economic development of Germany, its largest trading partner. According to the data of the Federal Statistical Office of Germany, the German economy has stagnated since the second quarter of 2019, and the annual economic growth was only 0.6%, the lowest since 2013.

By sectors, industry, especially manufacturing, accounted for the largest share of the Czech GDP, which was consistent with its industrial base. As shown in Figure 2-2, in 2019, the Czech gross industrial output value was CZK 1,515.591 billion (equivalent to USD 66.085 billion), accounting for 26.4% of GDP, of which the manufacturing industry created an output value of CZK 1,286.547 billion (equivalent to USD 56.098 billion), accounting for 22.4% of GDP. The specific industries such as automobile manufacturing, mechanical equipment and metal products had great contribution. Followed by wholesale and retail, transportation, accommodation and catering, accounted for 16.8% of GDP, and then public administration, education, health and social work, accounted for 13.9%. Compared with 2018, the proportion of construction industry, information and communication industry, real estate industry, professional science and technology, management service industry, public administration, education, health and social work in the share of GDP in 2019 were increased.

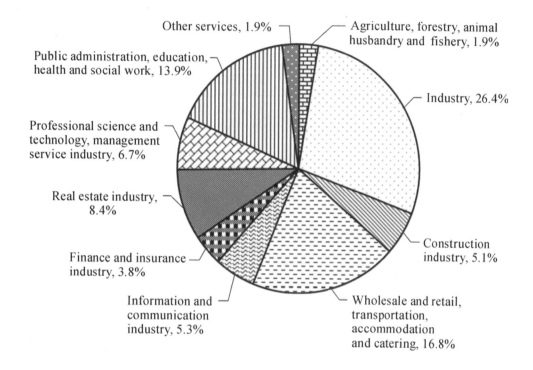

Figure 2-2　Distribution of Czech GDP Industry in 2019

(**Source:** Czech Statistical Office)

Note: Industries include mining, manufacturing and the production and supply of electricity, heat, gas and water.

2. The Domestic Demand Contributed More to Economic Growth, among which Household Consumption Was Still Strong and Had Its Own Dynamic

The domestic demand is an important engine of Czech economic growth. As shown in Table 2-1, the domestic demand volume of the Czech Republic in 2019 was CZK 5,402,284 million (equivalent to USD 235,558 million), which actually increased by 2.5% and contributed 98.1% to GDP growth.

36

Development Report on Zhejiang-Czech Economic and Trade
Cooperation under the Framework of the Belt and Road Initiative (2020)

Table 2-1   Contribution of the Czech Domestic Demand to GDP in 2019

Demand item	Scale (CZK 100 million)	Growth rate (%)	Contribution rate (%)
Total domestic demand	54,022.84	2.5	98.1
●Consumer expenditure	38,548.12	2.8	80.0
▲Household consumption expenditure	26,703.41	2.9	58.7
▲Government consumption expenditure	11,346.57	2.3	18.2
●Capital formation	15,474.72	1.5	17.8
▲Formation of fixed capital	15,069.14	2.2	24.7

(**Source:** Czech Statistical Office)

Note: The contribution rate was calculated according to the ratio of constant price demand increment to GDP increment in 2015.

By consumption, the household consumption demand remained strong, while the growth of government consumption demand slowed down. In 2019, the total consumption expenditure of the Czech Republic reached CZK 3,854.812 billion (equivalent to USD 168.083 billion), an actual increase of 2.8%, accounting for 67.1% of the total GDP. Among them, household consumption expenditure reached CZK 2,670.341 billion (equivalent to USD 116.436 billion), accounting for 69.3% of total consumption expenditure, with an actual increase of 2.9%. Government consumption expenditure was CZK 1,134.657 billion (equivalent to USD 49.475 billion), which actually increased by 2.3% and decreased by 1.5% compared with that in 2018. In terms of contribution, the contribution rate of total consumption expenditure to GDP growth in the whole year reached 80.0%, 6.3 % higher than that in 2018, which was the highest contribution rate in recent three years, which drove the GDP growth by 1.9%. Among them, the contribution rate of household consumption expenditure accounted for 58.7%, 10.6 % higher than that in 2018, driving GDP growth by 1.4%. According to the data of economic confidence index (monthly) released by Czech Statistical Office, the monthly average of consumer confidence index in 2019 reached 110.1, which was lower than 116.9 in 2018, but still at a relatively high level.

By investment, the growth rate of investment demand slowed down obviously, and the contribution of economic growth declined greatly. In 2019, the total of Czech capital formation was CZK 1,547.472 billion (equivalent to USD 67.475 billion), with an actual increase of 1.5%, which was 6.2 % lower than that in 2018. Among them, the fixed capital amounted to CZK 1,506.914 billion (equivalent to USD 65.707 billion), with an actual increase of 2.2% and a decrease of 7.8 %, compared with 2018. Machinery and equipment, buildings and intellectual property products were the main categories of fixed capital formation, and these three categories accounted for 80.2% of the total capital formation, exceeding 4/5. From the aspect of contribution, the contribution rate of total new investment to GDP growth was 17.8%, which was the lowest contribution rate in recent three years, and the contribution rate of fixed capital formation was 24.7%, far lower than 78.9% in 2018, which drove GDP growth by 0.6%.

3. The Growth Rate of Import and Export Has Turned from Positive to Negative with High Concentration of Trade Countries and Commodities

In 2019, influenced by external uncertainties such as Sino-US trade war and Brexit, the import and export trade volume of Czech goods declined relatively compared with that in 2018, and the growth rate turned from positive to negative. As shown in Figure 2-3, the total import and export trade of goods in the Czech Republic in 2019 was USD 378.818 billion, down 2.3% year-on-year. Among them, exports were USD 199.417 billion, down 1.6% year-on-year. Imports reached USD 179.401 billion, down 3.1% year-on-year. The trade surplus was USD 20.016 billion, a year-on-year increase of 13.4%, which was larger than that in 2018. Looking back the past years, Czech goods import and export trade has developed rapidly, which was higher than the average annual growth rate of GDP (3.3%). From 2015 to 2019, the import and export trade volume of Czech goods increased from USD 299.247 billion to USD 378.818 billion with an average annual growth rate of 6.1%. Among them, exports increased from USD 157.880 billion to USD 199.417 billion, with an average annual growth rate of 6.0%. Imports increased from USD 141.366 billion to USD 179.401 billion, with an average annual growth rate of 6.1%.

In terms of trade countries, more than 70% of Czech goods trade was carried out in the EU. In 2019, the Czech Republic's exports to the EU (28 countries, statistics still included the United Kingdom) were USD 166.762 billion, accounting for 83.6% of its total exports; imports from the EU (28 countries) amounted to USD 112.062 billion, accounting for 62.5% of its total exports. In terms of specific countries, Germany was the traditional trade market of the Czech Republic, and the trade volume between the two sides accounted for more than 1/4 of the total import and export trade of Czech goods. In 2019, the top five Czech export target countries were Germany (31.8%), Slovakia (7.6%), Poland (6.0%), France (5.1%) and the United Kingdom (4.5%); the top five importing countries were Germany (24.7%), China (15.8%), Poland (7.5%), Slovakia (4.4%) and Italy (4.1%). China was the 17th export target country and the 2nd import source country of the Czech Republic. The Czech Republic exported USD 2.471 billion of goods to China in the whole year, a year-on-year decrease of 4.4%. Imported goods from China reached USD 28.294 billion, a year-on-year increase of 8.6%. The trade deficit reached

38

Development Report on Zhejiang-Czech Economic and Trade
Cooperation under the Framework of the Belt and Road Initiative (2020)

USD 25.823 billion, achieving a third consecutive year of growth, and the growth amount was lowered than that in 2018.

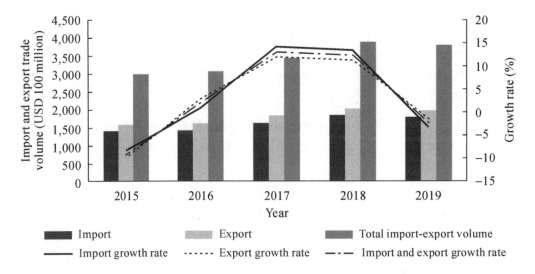

Figure 2-3　Czech Import and Export Trade Scale and Its Growth Rate from 2015 to 2019

(**Source:** Czech Statistical Office)

In terms of trade commodities, machinery and transportation equipment were the main trade categories in the Czech Republic. The top ten Czech export commodities in 2019 were shown in Table 2-2. The total export volume accounted for nearly 70% of the total Czech export volume in the same period, and the product concentration was high. Seven items belonged to the category of machinery and transportation equipment, among which five items of machinery and transportation equipment occupied the top five in exports, accounting for more than half of the total exports. The first export commodity reflected the important position of automobile industry in Czech national economy to a certain extent. According to the data released by the Czech Automotive Industry Association (AIA), in 2019, the Czech automobile production was 1,427,600, ranking first among Central and Eastern European Countries. The automobile industry accounted for more than 20% of Czech industrial production and export, and R&D investment accounted for one third.

As shown in Table 2-3, the top ten Czech imports in 2019 accounted for 60.5% of the total Czech imports in the same period, and the concentration of imported products was lower than that of exported products, but it was still at a high level. Six items belonged to the category of machinery and transportation equipment, among which five items of machinery and transportation equipment occupied the top five import positions, accounting for 41.2% of total imports. Nine items of the top ten commodities in import and export overlapped, among which the top five items were highly consistent, which showed that the Czech

Table 2-2 Top Ten Commodities Exported by the Czech Republic in 2019

SN	Name of commodity	Categories	Amount of money (USD 100 million)	Proportion (%)
1	Land vehicles (including air cushion type)	Machinery and transport equipment	403.22	20.2
2	Electric machinery, appliances and their electrical parts	Machinery and transport equipment	189.39	9.5
3	Telecommunications and sound recording and playback equipment	Machinery and transport equipment	157.26	7.9
4	Office machinery and automatic data processing equipment	Machinery and transport equipment	153.51	7.7
5	General industrial machinery equipment and parts	Machinery and transport equipment	138.99	7.0
6	Miscellaneous products	Miscellaneous products	103.95	5.2
7	Metal products	Finished products classified by raw materials	93.32	4.7
8	Special machinery for special industries	Machinery and transport equipment	54.94	2.8
9	Power machinery and equipment	Machinery and transport equipment	47.82	2.4
10	Iron and steel	Finished products classified by raw materials	46.18	2.3

(**Source:** Czech Statistical Office)

Note: Trade commodities are classified according to SITC (Standard International Trade Classification) two-digit code, the same below.

intra-industry trade ratio was significant, especially the import and export of machinery and transportation equipment were frequent. For China, in 2019, the Czech Republic mainly exports machinery and equipment and raw material products such as pulp and wood to China, and mainly imports machinery and equipment, clothing, metal products and other labor-intensive products from China.

Table 2-3   Top Ten Commodities Imported by the Czech Republic in 2019

SN	Name of commodity	Categories	Amount of money (USD 100 million)	Proportion (%)
1	Electric machinery, appliances and their electrical parts	Machinery and transport equipment	187.27	10.4
2	Land vehicles (including air cushion type)	Machinery and transport equipment	181.31	10.1
3	Telecommunications and sound recording and playback equipment	Machinery and transport equipment	157.98	8.8
4	Office machinery and automatic data processing equipment	Machinery and transport equipment	119.40	6.7
5	General industrial machinery equipment and parts	Machinery and transport equipment	93.86	5.2
6	Miscellaneous products	Miscellaneous products	80.95	4.5
7	Metal products	Finished products classified by raw materials	71.08	4.0
8	Iron and steel	Finished products classified by raw materials	70.85	3.9
9	Petroleum, petroleum products and related materials	Fossil fuels, lubricants and related raw materials	62.90	3.5
10	Power machinery and equipment	Machinery and transport equipment	60.75	3.4

(**Source:** Czech Statistical Office)

4. Inflation and Fiscal Deficit Were Rising, and Macroeconomic Policies Were under Pressure

As shown in Figure 2-4, the inflation rate in the Czech Republic in 2019 was 2.8%, which was 0.7% higher than that in 2018. It was a year with higher inflation rate in the Czech Republic in recent 11 years, only lower than 3.3% in 2012, which was mainly due to the rising prices of housing, food, health care, education, catering and accommodation in the Czech Republic in 2019. Since the inflation rate exceeded the target value by 2.0% in 2017, the Czech National Bank has continuously raised interest rates to curb the inflation rate from rising. In May 2019, the Czech National Bank raised the two-week repo rate, Lumbard interest rate and discount rate to 2.0%, 3.0% and 1.0% respectively, and predicted that the economy would gradually slow down and keep the above interest rates unchanged until the end of 2019.

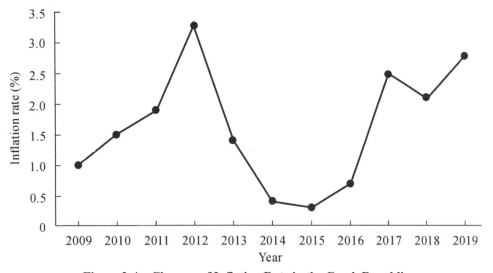

Figure 2-4   Changes of Inflation Rate in the Czech Republic

(**Source:** Czech Statistical Office)

In 2019, the Czech fiscal deficit was CZK 28.515 billion (equivalent to USD 1.240 billion), and the financial situation was the worst in the past four years—that year its fiscal revenue was CZK 1,523.200 billion (equivalent to USD 66.420 billion) and its fiscal expenditure was CZK 1,551.700 billion (equivalent to USD 67.660 billion). In the 2020 Czech Republic Government Budget, the annual budget deficit was CZK 40 billion, the budget revenue was CZK 1,578.300 billion and the budget expenditure was CZK 1,618.300 billion. The budget was given priority to rising pensions, teachers' salaries and family welfare. It is worth noting that the Czech Republic is one of the countries with the least debt in Europe. In 2019, the Czech government debt was CZK 1,640.185 billion (equivalent to

42

Development Report on Zhejiang-Czech Economic and Trade
Cooperation under the Framework of the Belt and Road Initiative (2020)

USD 71.518 billion), accounting for 28.5% of its GDP, 1.5 % lower than that in 2018—so the year 2019 was the seventh consecutive year of decline.

II. Forecast of Czech Economic Development Trend

1. Overall Trend

Affected by the COVID-19 pandemic and various bans, the Czech economy will fall into recession in 2020, and the growth rate will drop sharply (see Table 2-4). According to the latest forecast of the Czech National Bank in August 2020, the Czech economy is expected to shrink by 8.2% in 2020, which is 0.2% lower than the forecast in May, facing the worst recession since the founding of the country in 1993; in 2021, GDP will increase by 3.5%, a decrease of 0.5% from the previous forecast. Previously, many institutions had predicted the Czech economic growth in 2020 to varying degrees. The European Commission's *Summer Economic Forecast Report* released in July predicted that the Czech economy would decline by 7.8% in 2020. The World Economic Outlook Report released by the International Monetary Fund (IMF) in June predicted a decline of 6.5%. The Czech Ministry of Finance predicted a decline of 5.6% in April, and Deloitte predicted a decline of about 10.0% in March.

Table 2-4　Czech GDP Growth Forecast Adjustment (2018—2021)

Year	2018	2019	2020	2021	2020	2021
			Latest forecast		Previous forecast	
GDP growth rate (%)	3.2	2.3	−8.2	3.5	−8.0	4.0

(**Source:** Czech Statistical Office, Czech National Bank)

Note: The data in 2018 and 2019 are from the Czech Statistical Office; the data of 2020 and 2021 are from the Czech National Bank. The latest forecast data is the data in August 2020 and the previous forecast data is the data in May 2020.

In the first quarter of 2020, the Czech GDP fell by 1.7% year-on-year and 3.3% quarter-on-quarter, the largest decline since the second quarter of 2013; in the second quarter, it fell by 10.7% year-on-year and 8.4% quarter-on-quarter, the biggest decline since 1993. With the gradual relaxation of epidemic prevention and control measures in May, the economy is expected to recover in the third quarter, but the recovery will last for a long time. As shown in Figure 2-5, the economic confidence index of the Czech Republic fell continuously in the first four months of 2020, and began to rebound continuously after plunging 20 points in April. It rose to 86.7 points in July, but it was still far below the long-term average. Among them, the consumer confidence index was 96.0 points in July, an increase of 2.7 points from June, but still 8.8 points lower than that in January; the industrial confidence index rose the most in July, with a sharp increase of 19.8 points to 89.8 points, but still less than January; the confidence index of the construction industry dropped continuously from 123.9 points in January to 102.4 points in June, and it rose slightly to 103.0 points in July; the trade confidence index became the only sub-index that declined in July, dropping by 2.6 points to 89.5 points. With the effective control of the epidemic and the support of a series of economic stimulus policies, the economic decline will be narrowed in the third quarter, but the economic recovery in 2020 is still weak. Under the background of continuous efforts of various economic stimulus policies and low base in 2020, the Czech economy will rebound in 2021, but it will still be difficult to return to the pre-epidemic level, and the economic recovery will be slow.

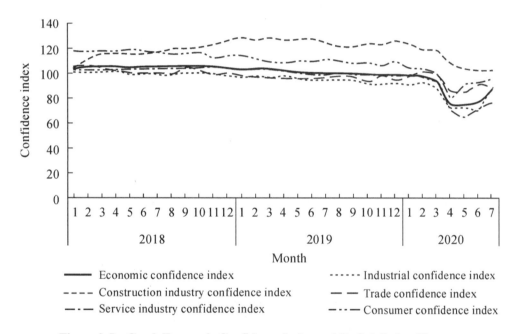

Figure 2-5   Czech Economic Confidence Index and Its Sub-Index Changes

(**Source:** Czech Statistical Office)

2. Favorable Factors

(1) Good Foundation for Economic Recovery

The Czech Republic is one of the first countries in the EU to introduce epidemic prevention and control measures, and also the first country in Central and Eastern Europe to announce deregulation. The early control of the epidemic gave the Czech Republic an

44

Development Report on Zhejiang-Czech Economic and Trade
Cooperation under the Framework of the Belt and Road Initiative (2020)

opportunity to reopen its market and helped the economy recover faster. The latest report of the *2020 Global Manufacturing Index* released by Cushman & Wakefield evaluated and ranked 48 major global manufacturing destinations in terms of operating conditions, manufacturing costs and risk composition. The results showed that, given its strategic geographical location, low geopolitical risk and comprehensive operating cost advantages, the Czech Republic ranked fourth (the top three are China, the United States and India), and ranked first in Europe, making it the most suitable European country for developing manufacturing industry. The report also predicted and evaluated the recovery ability of manufacturing industries in various countries under the COVID-19 pandemic. The results showed that China and other four Asia-Pacific countries ranked in the first tier among countries that are most likely to restart manufacturing industries, and the Czech Republic was in the second tier. The *Global Competitiveness Report 2020* released by International Institute for Management Development (IMD) in Lausanne, Switzerland, evaluated and ranked 63 countries and regions around the world in terms of economic performance, government efficiency, business efficiency and infrastructure. The results showed that the Czech Republic ranked 33rd and was the most competitive country in Central and Eastern Europe. However, there are some shortcomings in infrastructure, labor market and digitalization. In order to consolidate the advantages and make up for weaknesses, the Czech government actively plans a medium and long-term economic development strategy. In January 2020, it approved a document on the key points of the national economic strategy by 2030, focusing on eight key areas: industry, construction and raw materials, transportation, energy, education and labor market, commerce and trade, R&D, innovation and digitalization, regional, rural and agriculture, and health care. The main goal is to make the Czech Republic one of the 20 most competitive economies the world by 2030.

(2) Strong Support for Investment and Development

Since the release of *Digital Czech Republic v. 2.0—The Way to the Digital Economy* in 2018 and *Innovation Strategy of the Czech Republic 2019—2030: The Country for the Future* in 2019, the Czech government has made great efforts to plan corresponding project plans and funds to provide strong support for the sustained growth of investment. On September 6, 2019, a new investment incentive policy was implemented, and more attention was expected to be paid to high-tech and high value-added investment projects. In June 2020, the Czech government approved the "Digital Czech Project Implementation Plan for 2020—2021", with an estimated expenditure of CZK 2.47 billion (approx. USD 100 million). The primary goal is to achieve government digital services. The Czech government is working out a national investment plan for the next 30 years, involving more than 20,000 projects and CZK 8 trillion (approx. USD 344.3 billion), of which transportation infrastructure projects account for 75%. At the same time, the Czech government is preparing to set up a national development fund to provide funding for investment projects that promote the social and economic development of the Czech Republic. In the initial stage, the four major commercial banks in the Czech Republic will invest CZK 7 billion to the fund. Early projects will focus on infrastructure, education and health care, including PPP (Public-Private Partnership) model investment projects. In addition, during the fight against the epidemic, the Czech President Miloš Zeman said that in order to solve the economic crisis, the country should focus on investment, of which the most effective investment is transportation and housing construction. After attending the EU summit, the Czech Prime Minister Andrej Babiš stated that the Czech Republic will receive subsidies of EUR 8.7 billion from the EU COVID-19 Economic Recovery Fund, and the budget of EUR 27 billion in the EU "Multiannual Financial Framework 2021—2027", meaning that the Czech Republic will receive EUR 35.7 billion from EU funds in the next seven years. The Czech plans to use EU funds to support investment in automobile industry, health care and digitalization, which will help Czech economic recovery and development.

(3) Favorable Economic Stimulus Policy

In response to the impact of the epidemic, the Czech Republic quickly adopted a proactive fiscal policy and an expansionary monetary policy to support the economy. In terms of fiscal policy, the annual budget deficit was revised three times in 2020. In March, it was raised from CZK 40 billion at the beginning of the year to 200 billion, in April to 300 billion, and in June to 500 billion, setting a historical record. The highest budget deficit was CZK 192.4 billion in 2009. Among them, the budget revenue decreased CZK 213.3 billion to CZK 1,365.0 billion, and the budget expenditure increased CZK 246.7 billion to CZK 1,865.0 billion. According to the data released by the Czech Ministry of Finance, as of June 2020, the Czech fiscal deficit reached CZK 195.2 billion. Among them, fiscal revenue was CZK 699.7 billion, a year-on-year decrease of CZK 44.2 billion; fiscal expenditure was CZK 894.9 billion, a year-on-year increase of CZK 130.4 billion. The expenditure of direct measures taken by the government to deal with the impact of the epidemic is CZK 86.5 billion, the expenditure of purchasing protective gears, paying national insurance and paying off debts for some hospitals is CZK 21.4 billion, and the assistance provided by loan guarantee is CZK 32.6 billion. In the first half of 2020, the total Czech government debt was CZK 2.16 trillion, an increase of CZK 516.7 billion year-on-year. This is mainly due to the issuance of government bonds to make up for the budget deficit. In terms of monetary policy, after raising interest rates nine times since 2017, the Czech Central Bank cut interest rates in March and May 2020, after the epidemic. The two-week repo rate was reduced to 0.25%, returning to the low interest level in 2012, which will help reduce loan costs, stimulate investment and consumption willingness and boost economic recovery.

46

Development Report on Zhejiang-Czech Economic and Trade
Cooperation under the Framework of the Belt and Road Initiative (2020)

3. Unfavorable Factors

(1) Weak and Uncertain External Demand

The world economy shows a slow and fragile recovery, with weak demand for trade and investment and high uncertainty. The IMF predicted that the global economy would shrink by 4.9% in 2020, the worst recession since the Great Depression; the annual growth rate of major developed economies would decline sharply, and the United States, the United Kingdom and the Eurozone would decline by 8%, 10.2% and 10.2% respectively. Among them, Germany's GDP, the largest trade market of the Czech Republic, would decline by 7.8% in 2020. The World Trade Organization (WTO) updated its global outlook report in June, predicting that global merchandise trade would fall sharply by 13% in 2020. According to preliminary statistics, the first and second quarters of global merchandise trade declined by 3% and 18.5% year-on-year respectively. The *World Investment Report* released by the United Nations Conference on Trade and Development (UNCTAD) in June predicts that the global foreign direct investment (FDI) in 2020 would be less than USD 1 trillion, a decrease of 40% year-on-year, reaching the lowest level since 2005; it will further decrease by 5% to 10% in 2021 and begin to recover in 2022. Under the background of global economic recession, investment and consumption demands in various countries are generally weak, and the recovery of Czech's external demand market is weak and full of uncertainties, which mainly depends on the duration of the pandemic and the effectiveness of policies. In addition, external unstable factors such as the escalation of trade protectionism, the decline of Sino-US relations and Brexit will not change fundamentally in the short term, which will cause collateral effects and increase the difficulty of the Czech economic and trade recovery.

(2) Downturn in Domestic Market Segments

The pandemic prevention measures restricting the movement of people have brought a direct blow to international transportation and tourism, which have been affected throughout the year. The downturn in Czech domestic automobile manufacturing, tourism and other market segments may last longer. Taking the automobile industry, the pillar industry of Czech economy, as an example, during the epidemic, three automobile manufacturers, such as Skoda Auto of Czech, Hyundai Motor Company of Korea and Toyota Peugeot Citroën Automobile, all suffered production suspension that caused huge economic losses. According to the data released by the Czech Automotive Industry Association (AIA), the output of passenger cars in the Czech Republic in the first half of 2020 was 503,615, a year-on-year decrease of 32.6%, among which the output of Skoda, Hyundai and Peugeot Citroën decreased by 28.2%, 40.0% and 40.3% respectively. The annual output was expected to recover to 60%-90% of that before the epidemic. In April, the month with the longest downtime, the monthly output dropped by 88.5% year-on-year. According to the data of Czech Car Importers Association (CIA), in the first half of 2020, the sales passenger cars in the Czech Republic was 95,029, a year-on-year decrease of 26%, with the largest drop of 76.3% in April. Affected by the epidemic, both the supply and demand of the automobile industry have decreased significantly, and the market has shrunk severely. The industry faces the dual challenges of restructuring the supply chain on the supply side and reshaping consumer confidence on the demand side, and there are certain interim difficulties.

(3) Restricted Labor Mobility

The restrictions on labor mobility caused by the epidemic prevention and control measures have aggravated the shortage of employment in the Czech labor market, facing a decline in employment and rising wages. According to data released by the Czech Statistical Office, in the first and second quarters of 2020, the number of employed people in the Czech Republic decreased by 0.9% and 2.1% year-on-year, respectively, which was the first decline since 2014. Since the average monthly salary hit a record high of CZK 34,111 (USD 1,487) in 2019, it reached CZK 34,077 (USD 1,459) in the first quarter of 2020, a real year-on-year increase of 1.4%. According to the data released by Eurostat, since the unemployment rate in the Czech Republic hit a record low of 2.0% in 2019, it has remained at this level until April 2020. It rose slightly to 2.4% and 2.6% in May and June respectively, which is still the country with the lowest unemployment rate in the EU. Even during the epidemic, the unemployment rate did not deteriorate significantly. This was partly due to the timely remedial measures taken by the government, which also indicated a labor shortage. In response to the problem of labor shortage, the Czech Republic has introduced a large number of foreign laborers. At the end of 2019, the government also decided to double the Ukrainian labor quota to alleviate the problem of labor shortage. However, due to the spread of the epidemic, it was not implemented smoothly.

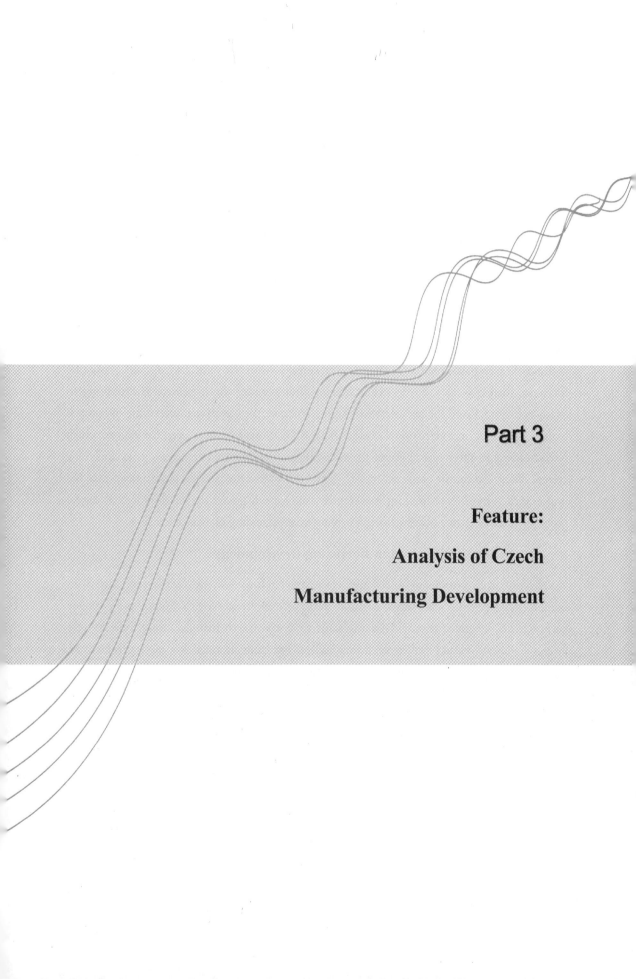

Part 3

Feature:

Analysis of Czech

Manufacturing Development

50

Development Report on Zhejiang-Czech Economic and Trade
Cooperation under the Framework of the Belt and Road Initiative (2020)

Introduction

◆ Current Situation of Czech Manufacturing Development

The scale of the Czech manufacturing industry ranks first among all industries, with its value-added contribution to GDP accounting for more than 20%, which forms a strong support for economic growth. From the perspective of industry structure, the Czech manufacturing industry focuses on developing high-tech industries such as automobile manufacturing, mechanical equipment, electrical and electronics, etc. Among them, automobile manufacturing has outstanding advantages, with the value-added scale accounting for more than one-fifth of the manufacturing industry and the increment contributing to nearly one-third. From the perspective of trade structure, the Czech manufacturing industry is highly dependent on international trade. About 85% of its output is used for export, which has considerable international competitiveness, highly concentrated trade countries and trade commodities. From the perspective of digital progress, the Czech government attaches importance to modern technology and services, and actively guides the development of digital economy, making digital transformation promote the upgrading of manufacturing.

◆ Vision for Czech Manufacturing Development

Manufacturing industry is an important driving force of the Czech economy, with unique development advantages, mainly reflected in technological innovation, policy environment, integrated cost, etc. At the same time, the Czech manufacturing industry also faces many problems and challenges, mainly reflected in labor shortage, low labor productivity, declining corporate profit margins, etc. In order to improve the competitiveness in the fourth industrial revolution, the Czech Republic puts forward the "Průmysl 4.0 (Industry 4.0) Initiative", which is committed to improving the automation, intelligence and digitalization of the manufacturing industry, boosting its economic transformation and upgrading. At present, the weak international market demand has severely hampered the Czech economy, and the manufacturing industry bears the brunt. The COVID-19 pandemic has become the biggest threat to the recovery of the Czech manufacturing industry. In addition, the escalation of trade protectionism, the Brexit, Sino-US relations, and European-American trade relations will also increase uncertainty. Therefore, the future development of the Czech manufacturing industry will be largely influenced by the external international environment.

The Czech Republic is a traditional industrial country with a long industrial history. The manufacturing industry plays an important role in the Czech national economy and makes positive contributions to economic growth, technological progress, employment increase, etc. As a member of the European Union, the Czech Republic advocates a free trade policy, and the manufacturing industry has certain competitiveness in the international market, especially in the fields of automobile manufacturing, mechanical equipment, electrical and electronics. In 2019, the Czech manufacturing exports accounted for more than 85% of its output and more than 90% of goods exports, which was an important source of trade surplus. The Czech manufacturing industry has advantages in technological innovation, policy environment and integrated cost, but it also faces problems such as labor shortage, low labor productivity and declining corporate profit margins. In 2020, affected by the COVID-19 pandemic, the Czech economy is severely hampered by the weak demand at home and abroad. The manufacturing production and trade will shrink sharply, so various external risk factors should be paid attention to during this period.

I . Current Situation of Czech Manufacturing Development

1. The Manufacturing Industry Ranks First among All Industries

The Czech Republic is a traditional industrial country whose manufacturing industry occupies an important position in the national economy and makes important contributions to Czech economy. As shown in Figure 3-1, from 2010 to 2019, the Czech manufacturing value added increased from CZK 836.893 billion (USD 43.791 billion) to CZK 1,286.547 billion (USD 56.098 billion), with an average annual growth rate of 3.8% at constant prices in 2015, which is 1.4 percentage points higher than the average annual GDP growth level (2.4%) in the same period. It accounts for more than 20% of GDP, ranking first among all industries, and providing a strong support for GDP growth. In the past decade, the proportion of manufacturing in the Czech industries has been on the rise, with the proportion of value added having gradually increased from 78.2% in 2010 to 84.9% in 2019. In 2019, the Czech manufacturing value added actually increased by 3.1% year-on-year, accounting for 22.4% of the annual GDP. There include more than 180,000 enterprises, most of which are small- and medium-sized enterprises; there are more than 1.31 million employees, accounting for 28.1% of the total employment, more than one fourth, and maintaining the position of the largest employer in the industry. According to the Eurostat data, the Czech manufacturing output index reached 114.9 in 2019, higher than the average level of EU countries (106.1).

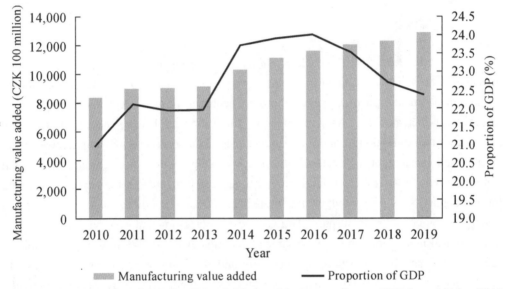

Figure 3-1   Czech Manufacturing Value Added and Its Proportion to GDP from 2010 to 2019

(**Source:** Czech Statistical Office)

2. Focus on the Development of High-Tech Industries

In terms of the value-added scale, the top ten manufacturing industries in the Czech Republic in 2019 are shown in Figure 3-2, with the total value added accounting for 79.2% of the annual GDP. Among them, the manufacture of motor vehicles, trailers and semi-trailers is the largest category of the manufacturing industry. In 2019, its value added reached CZK 271.231 billion (USD 11.827 billion), accounting for 21.1% of the manufacturing industry. It is followed by the manufacture of fabricated metal products, except machinery and equipment and manufacture of machinery and equipment n.e.c. (not elsewhere classified). Their value added accounted for 11.7% and 8.5% of the manufacturing industry respectively, which were far behind the first major manufacture of motor vehicles, trailers and semi-trailers. In the past decade, the overall structure of the manufacturing industry has not changed much. The total value added of the top ten industries has kept stable at about 78%, but the internal structure was obviously divided, with the different changes in the proportion of various industries. Among them, the proportion of the manufacture of motor vehicles, trailers and semi-trailers rose the fastest, from 17.9% in 2010 to 21.1% in 2019, an increase of 3.2 percentage points, followed by the manufacture of fabricated metal products, except machinery and equipment, and manufacture of chemicals and chemical products, which increased by 1.3 and 0.9 percentage points respectively. The proportion of the manufacture of food products declined the fastest, from 6.4% in 2010 to 5.3% in 2019, a decrease of 1.1 percentage points, followed by a decrease of 1.1 percentage point in the proportion of the manufacture of machinery and equipment n.e.c.

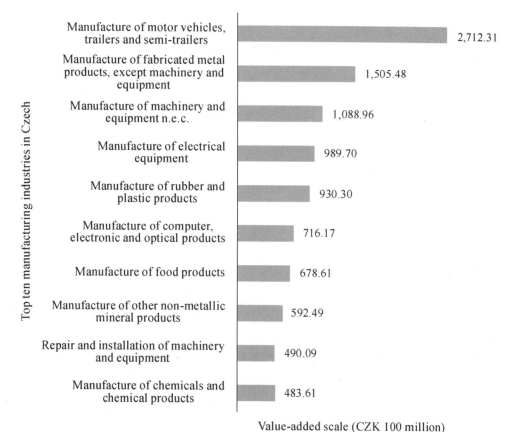

Value-added scale (CZK 100 million)

Figure 3-2   Top Ten Industries of Czech Manufacturing Value-Added Scale in 2019

(**Source:** Czech Statistical Office)

Note: Czech manufacturing sub-sectors are classified according to CZ-NACE, mainly including 24 secondary industries such as food, beverage, tobacco, textile, leather, wood processing, chemical industry, medicine, rubber, metallurgy, electronics, machinery, automobile and furniture, the same below.

54

Development Report on Zhejiang-Czech Economic and Trade
Cooperation under the Framework of the Belt and Road Initiative (2020)

From the perspective of incremental contribution, the top ten industries contributing to the growth of Czech manufacturing industry from 2010 to 2019 are shown in Table 3-1. The total incremental contribution was as high as 95.5%, of which the mechanical equipment category exceeded 60%. The contribution of the manufacture of motor vehicles, trailers and semi-trailers to the increment of manufacturing value added was the highest, 32.2%, nearly one third of the whole. Next came the manufacture of fabricated metal products, except machinery and equipment, manufacture of electrical equipment, manufacture of computer, electronic and optical products, with incremental contributions all exceeding 10%.

**Table 3-1   Top Ten Industries Contributing to the Czech Manufacturing
Value-Added Increment from 2010 to 2019**

SN	Industry name	Incremental contribution	SN	Industry name	Incremental contribution
1	Manufacture of motor vehicles, trailers and semi-trailers	32.2%	6	Manufacture of rubber and plastic products	5.9%
2	Manufacture of fabricated metal products, except machinery and equipment	12.5%	7	Manufacture of machinery and equipment n.e.c.	4.7%
3	Manufacture of electrical equipment	12.5%	8	Manufacture of food products	3.9%
4	Manufacture of computer, electronic and optical products	10.6%	9	Manufacture of other non-metallic mineral products	3.1%
5	Manufacture of chemicals and chemical products	7.0%	10	Other manufacturing	3.1%

(**Source:** Czech Statistical Office)

Note: The incremental contribution is calculated according to the ratio of the incremental value added of each industry and the incremental value added of manufacturing industry at constant price in 2015.

In terms of the actual growth rate, from 2010 to 2019, the manufacture of chemicals and chemical products (7.0%) had the fastest average annual growth rate of value added calculated at constant prices in 2015, 3.2 percentage points higher than the average annual growth rate of the manufacturing industry. It was followed by manufacture of computer, electronic and optical products, manufacture of electrical equipment and manufacture of motor vehicles, trailers and semi-trailers, with an average annual increase of 6.4%, 6.4%, and 5.5% respectively. The above-mentioned fast-growing industries all belong to high-tech fields, while the growth rate of value added of labor-intensive industries such as textiles and garments showed a downward trend. In 2019, the value added of the manufacture of textiles, manufacture of leather and related products declined by 5.8% and 7.9% respectively, which also reflected the labor shortage in the Czech Republic to a certain extent.

In terms of the value-added scale, incremental contribution and actual growth rate, automobile manufacturing, metal products, mechanical equipment, electrical and electronic, pharmaceutical and chemical industries are the dominant industries of the Czech manufacturing industry, mostly in the fields of high technology and high value added.

(1) Automobile Manufacturing Industry

Automobile manufacturing industry is the pillar industry of Czech national economy. Representative automobile manufacturers in the Czech Republic include Skoda Auto, Toyota Peugeot Citroën Automobile and Hyundai Motor Company. According to the data released by Czech Automotive Industry Association (AIA), in 2019, the output of passenger cars in the Czech Republic reached 1,427,600, among which Skoda ranked first, with 907,900 vehicles, a year-on-year increase of 2.5%. Hyundai and Toyota Peugeot Citroën produced 309,500 and 210,000 vehicles respectively. According to the Czech Car Importers Association (CIA), in 2019, the sales volume of cars in the Czech Republic was 249,900, a year-on-year decline of 4.4%, among which Skoda sold 85,895 cars, a year-on-year growth of 2%. In addition, there are hundreds of auto parts manufacturing suppliers in the Czech Republic and half of the top 50 global auto parts enterprises have invested in the Czech Republic, which has formed an automobile industry chain based on parts, components and end products. Skoda Group leads local enterprises and foreign-funded enterprises to cooperate with each other in production, making it one of the countries with the highest concentration of automobile manufacturing, design and R&D in the world. In order to improve the overall competitiveness of the automobile industry, the CzechInvest has set up a database of auto parts suppliers (www.automotive.czechinvest.org). In 2018, the European Union has approved regulations to limit the carbon dioxide emissions of passenger cars, which was a turning point for the whole European and global automobile industry, but it also meant the rise of hybrid and electric vehicles, and the importance of the development of autonomous vehicle systems in the future. The transformation of automobile industry is a great test for manufacturers, supply chains and infrastructure construction.

(2) Machinery Manufacturing Industry

With a long history and solid foundation, the machinery manufacturing industry is one of the most important manufacturing industries in the Czech Republic, covering power equipment, chemical equipment, food machinery, construction machinery, agricultural and forestry machinery, machine tools, mining machinery, metallurgical machinery, rubber and plastic processing machinery, textile machinery, printing machinery, leather processing machinery, etc. After more than ten years of reorganization and the introduction of foreign capital, the technical level and quality of Czech machinery manufacturing products have improved significantly. At present, Czech machine tools, power station equipment, boilers, mining machinery, food machinery, environmental protection equipment, textile machinery, military products, etc. have strong international competitiveness. Among them, Czech machine tool industry has a history of more than 150 years, ranking 7th in Europe and 12th in the world with its excellent quality and advanced design. Famous Czech machine tool brands include Tos Varnsdorf, Škoda, Mas, Zps, Ždas, etc. Information about Czech machine tools and forming machines enterprises can be found on the website of Czech Mechanical Technology Association (www.sst.cz).

(3) Electrical and Electronic Manufacturing Industry

Electrical and electronic manufacturing industry is one of the most competitive manufacturing industries in the Czech Republic, with a wide variety of products, including four major industries: 1) high-current electrical technology; 2) computers; 3) radio, television and communication equipment; 4) instruments and automation equipment. Electrical manufacturing accounts for more than 14% of Czech manufacturing output, and most of the industrial output is mainly exported to the EU market. Foxconn, Panasonic, Acer, Siemens and many other internationally renowned enterprises have set up factories and representative offices in the Czech Republic. In recent years, Czech computer industry has developed rapidly, and almost all products are sold to the distribution centers of multinational companies in Europe. Foxconn, Fic and Asus produce more than 4 million computers in the Czech Republic every year, making the Czech Republic one of the largest computer producers in Europe.

(4) Pharmaceutical Industry

Pharmaceutical industry, with great development potential, is regarded as one of the major industrial sectors with great importance and high R&D investment in the world. Czech pharmaceutical industry didn't become an independent industry until the end of the 19th century. After decades of rapid development, it has become a high-tech industry in the field of high value added industries. Due to the complexity and high cost of drug research and development, the main developers are large and medium-sized enterprises and foreign-funded enterprises that produce original drugs. Drugs for cardiovascular diseases and adjuvant chemotherapy produced in the Czech Republic are at the world advanced level, and the biotechnology for cancer treatment is also worthy of attention. The Czech Republic has a complete network of biotechnology research institutions, whose biotechnology, molecular biology and medicine R&D centers are mainly located in Prague and Olomouc, Hradec Králové, Pilsen, Budějovice, Brno and other big cities. Among them, Brno is well-known in the field of cardiovascular disease and cancer research, developing into a hub of biotechnology companies of the Czech Republic with the strong support of the local government. In order to cope with the adverse effects of the COVID-19 pandemic, the Czech government has given certain guidance to the direction of corporate investment, encouraged the priority investment in industries that are critical to containing the spread of the virus, and increased R&D and expenditure in the fields of medicine and drug research.

(5) Chemical industry

Chemical industry is one of the most advanced and fastest-growing industries in the Czech Republic, occupying an important position in the Czech economy. Chemical industry, the important supplier of raw materials, is closely linked to other manufacturing such as automobile, plastic and rubber, textile, electronics, construction, and paper industry. Czech chemical industry is highly developed, mainly producing polyethylene, polypropylene and styrene. It is the largest supplier and producer in the European Union. The chemical industry in the manufacturing sphere is one of the most important industries in the Czech Republic, with strong innovation capacity and great export potential.

(6) Aviation Industry

With a hundred-year tradition, the aviation industry in the Czech Republic is advantageous in professional continuity and internationalization. The Czech Republic is one of the few countries in Europe capable of developing and producing complete aircraft and aircraft parts on their own. At the same time, Czech aviation industry has become part of the supply chain of large global companies such as Airbus and Boeing. Czech aviation business is mainly divided into two parts: the first part is the production of complete aircraft, involving small aircraft suitable for local and regional transportation, trainers and light fighters, sports aircraft and agricultural aircraft, ultralight aircraft and gliders. Being the second producer of ultralight aircraft in Europe after Germany, the Czech Republic is home to a quarter of the ultralight aircraft sold worldwide. The second part is the production of aircraft parts for large transport aircraft, military aircraft and helicopters. The Czech Republic produces an average of 550 light aircraft, sports aircraft and 1,400 propellers every year with full intellectual property rights. More than 80% of the products are exported and mainly to EU countries. The Central Bohemian Region is the most concentrated area of aircraft manufacturing in the Czech Republic. The largest companies in Czech aviation industry include AERO Vodochody and Evektor-Aerotechnik. Developed and manufactured independently by the Czech Republic, Shark, one kind of light aircraft, enjoys world-renowned reputation. Adopting carbon fiber epoxy resin composite material as fuselage and incorporating shark bionics for streamline design which resembles shark shape, it is the world's fastest ultra-light aircraft.

(7) Nanotechnology

The Czech Republic is at the forefront of development in the field of nanotechnology in

58

Development Report on Zhejiang-Czech Economic and Trade
Cooperation under the Framework of the Belt and Road Initiative (2020)

the world. It not only has a group of powerful nanotechnology research institutions such as the Central European Institute of Technology (CEITEC), the Regional Center of Advanced Technologies and Materials (RCPTM) and the Institute for Nanomaterials, Advanced Technology and Innovation (CXI), but also owns a number of representative enterprises such as Elmarco, Synpo, Crytur and Optaglio. For example, Elmarco realized the industrialized operation of Nanospider, the world's first electrospinning nanofiber production line in 2006. As the world's first supplier of industrial production equipment for nanofibers, it has promoted the development of high-tech products such as filter membranes for purifying water and air and functional textile fabrics, creating favorable conditions for other Czech enterprises to professionally process nanofibers. During the outbreak of COVID-19, Batist Medicalas, one of the largest suppliers of masks and protective equipment in the Czech Republic, also applied nanotechnology to mask manufacturing. With a broad application prospect, nanotechnology exerts enormous influence in the fields of machinery, automobile, aviation, electronics, textile, biotechnology, surface treatment, purification and filtration, etc. It is a priority field for foreign investment in the Czech Republic. More detailed information of the development of nanotechnology in the Czech Republic can be obtained on the website www.nanotechnologie.cz.

(8) Glass and Ceramics Industry

As one of the traditional industries in the Czech Republic, glass and ceramics industry is renowned across the globe for its unique and top-quality handmade production. There are about 150 enterprises (mainly export-oriented) whose products are distributed in more than 180 countries around the world and most of which are exported to the European Union. The products with the largest market share are flat glass and its deep processing products, followed by glass packaging, glass fiber production and household glass. Czech glass and ceramics manufacturers are the most influential manufacturers in the industry. They pay attention to environmental protection, actively implement the concept of sustainable development, focus on R&D and investing in modern production, develop new technologies and processes for glass and ceramics manufacturing, and continue to simplify production processes and open up new export markets.

(9) Beer Brewing Industry

The beer brewing industry occupies an important position in the food industry of the Czech Republic. The first beer brewery in the Czech Republic was built in 1118 with time-honored beer brands such as Herold, Bernard and Pilsner. With a local climate suitable for cultivating hops, the per capita beer consumption in the Czech Republic ranks first in the world. The Czech Republic is a major producer and consumer of beer, and its main export targets are EU countries, especially Slovakia, Germany and Poland. Exports to EU countries account for about 80% of Czech beer exports.

3. Highly Dependent on International Trade

The Czech Republic joined the European Union in 2004. It advocated free trade policies, encouraged foreign direct investment and deeply participated in regional and global value chains. Its manufacturing industry has considerable competitiveness in the international market. Comparing with CZ-NACE, the Statistical Classification of Economic Activities of Czech Statistical Office with the Standard International Trade Classification or SITC, the manufacturing industry of the Czech Republic mainly includes chemicals and related products (section 5), manufactured products mainly classified by materials (section 6), machinery and transport equipment (section 7), and other miscellaneous manufactured articles (section 8) (see Figure 3-3). According to the trade statistics of these four categories, the import and export trade of Czech manufacturing industry reached USD 338.393 billion in 2019, a 2.0% drop year-on-year. Among them, exports were USD 182.818 billion, down 1.5% year-on-year; imports reached USD 155.575 billion, down 2.6% year-on-year.

In terms of manufacturing output share, in 2019, Czech manufacturing output was CZK 4,795.577 billion (USD 209.103 billion), and the proportion of exports reached 87.4%. It is evident that the development of Czech manufacturing largely benefited from the international market.

In terms of the share of goods trade, Czech manufacturing accounted for 89.3% of the total import and export of goods in 2019, of which exports accounted for 91.7% and imports accounted for 86.7%. It is obvious that Czech goods trade is dominated by manufacturing.

In terms of trade balance, Czech manufacturing industry showed a surplus as a whole, with a trade surplus of USD 27.243 billion in 2019, a year-on-year increase of 5.3%. Due to successive years of trade surplus, the Czech Republic has relatively abundant foreign exchange reserves, creating favorable conditions to keep the relative stability of exchange rate and inflation of Czech Krone. Therefore, the Czech Republic is more capable of maintaining macroeconomic stability than other Central and Eastern European Countries in the medium and long term.

In terms of trading countries, most of Czech manufacturing foreign trade takes place in the EU region with a relatively high dependence on the German market. According to the statistics in "Part 2 Development" of this book, more than 70% of Czech goods trade was carried out in the EU, of which about 1/3 exports and 1/4 imports were carried out with Germany. The Czech Republic is an important part of German industrial supply chain, providing various components in manufacturing field for Germany and other developed countries of the European Union. The Czech government also encourages enterprises to actively explore markets outside the EU, gradually achieve market diversification to reduce their dependence on the EU market.

Development Report on Zhejiang-Czech Economic and Trade
Cooperation under the Framework of the Belt and Road Initiative (2020)

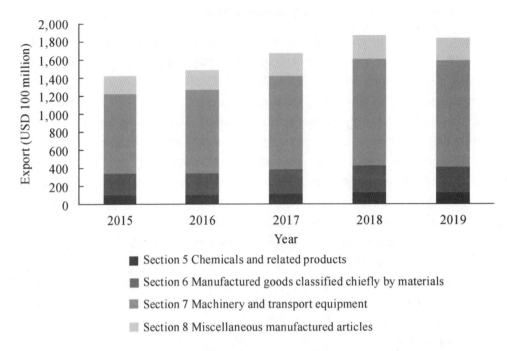

**Figure 3-3   Export Scale of SITC Main Sections of Czech Manufacturing Industry
from 2015 to 2019**

(**Source:** Czech Statistical Office)

In terms of trading commodities, automobiles, machinery and electrical equipment dominate. The 7th section of machinery and transport equipment is the largest section of manufacturing trade. In 2019, the export value was USD 117.472 billion and the import value was USD 86.369 billion, accounting for 64.3% and 55.5% of the manufacturing industry respectively. According to the statistics of SITC two-digit code in "Part 2 Development" of this book, the top five export and import commodities in the Czech Republic fall to the section of machinery and transport equipment, and the total exports and imports accounted for 57.0% and 47.6% of manufacturing respectively. In the 7th section of machinery and transport equipment, land vehicles (including air cushion type) displayed the largest trade surplus, reaching USD 22.191 billion, which is equivalent to 81.5% of the total trade surplus of the manufacturing industry. Table 3-2 gives a further analysis of SITC three-digit coded goods showing that automobiles and auto parts are the top two export commodities of the manufacturing industry. In 2019, exports were USD 37.929 billion, accounting for more than 20% of the total manufacturing export, which shows the pillar position of the automobile manufacturing industry.

Table 3-2 Top Ten Commodities Exported by Czech Manufacturing Industry in 2019

SN	Name of commodity	Major categories to which it belongs	Total amount (billion dollars)
1	Automobiles	Machinery and transport equipment	223.67
2	Automobile parts	Machinery and transport equipment	155.62
3	Automatic data processing machine and its devices	Machinery and transport equipment	130.70
4	Telecommunication equipment and its components	Machinery and transport equipment	129.38
5	Circuit switch	Machinery and transport equipment	60.77
6	Electric machine device	Machinery and transport equipment	51.21
7	Basic metal products	Manufactured goods classified chiefly by material	47.20
8	Furniture and its parts	Miscellaneous manufactured articles	42.57
9	Distribution equipment	Machinery and transport equipment	36.83
10	Baby strollers, toys, games and sporting goods	Miscellaneous manufactured articles	34.89

(**Source:** Czech Statistical Office)

Note: Trade commodities are classified according to SITC three-digit code.

Given the high concentration and close connection with foreign trade, Czech manufacturing industry is vulnerable to changes in the external environment. In 2019, Czech exports declined slightly due to the weak demand in Asian countries and the industrial recession in Germany. In the fourth quarter of 2019, Czech manufacturing output dropped by 2.2% owing to the weak demand of the pillar industry of automobile manufacturing industry.

4. Actively Guide the Development of Digitalization

The Czech government attaches great importance to modern technology and services, and strives to make the Czech Republic a leading country in the field of innovation and digitalization. In the process of manufacturing development, the Czech Republic is also committed to creating a new social environment and allowing digital transformation to promote manufacturing upgrading. In the past few years, the Czech government has actively guided the development of digital economy, frequently incorporated digitalization in various economic development strategic plans, which will bring new momentum to economic development and industrial upgrading. In February 2016, the Czech government approved the "National Plan for the Development of Next Generation Networks" (National Plan), which is committed to improving the broadband network coverage and speed. In October 2018, the Czech government approved the "Digital Strategy" and issued a cross-disciplinary strategic document *Digital Czech Republic v. 2.0—The Way to the Digital Economy* committed itself to promoting the digitalization process based on the three pillars (the Czech Republic under the background of digital Europe, digital public administration, digital economy and society). In February 2019, the Czech government approved the "National Innovation Strategy" and released the *Innovation Strategy of the Czech Republic 2019—2030: The Country for the Future*, proposing to build the Czech Republic into an innovation leader in Europe by 2030.

The Czech Innovation Strategy includes nine pillars, involving R&D, digitalization, intellectual property rights, smart investment and marketing. As part of the national innovation strategy, the Czech government approved the "National Artificial Intelligence (AI) Strategy" in May 2019, striving to build the Czech Republic into a model in the field of AI application in Europe. The strategic focus includes network security, industrial and manufacturing protection with the special attention of ensuring the safety of human beings in driverless vehicles, robots and automatic weapons. In response to the current low level of digitalization of the Czech national administrative services, the Chamber of Deputies passed the Digital Constitution at the end of 2019, which aimed to gradually realize the digitalization of national administrative processing and service provision while improving the efficiency of public administration. In June 2020, the Czech government approved the "Action Plan for Digital Czech Republic 2020—2021" with the primary goal of realizing digital government services.

In order to measure the progress of digitalization implementation, since 2017, the Czech Statistical Office has added some indicators such as Internet connection speed, cloud computing, 3D printing, robotics, big data, e-commerce and data exchange, to evaluate the digitalization level of the Czech Republic and the use of modern technology in various sectors of the national economy. In 2019, IMD released the third edition of the *World Digital*

Competitiveness Ranking. The results showed that given the relative backwardness in public administration efficiency and infrastructure construction progress, the digital competitiveness ranking of the Czech Republic among 63 economies in the world dropped from 29th in 2018 to 33rd. Through the evaluation of three factors: digital knowledge, digital technology and digital readiness, IMD's digital competitiveness aims to measure the capabilities and readiness of the economy to adopt and explore the use of digital technology to promote the transformation of enterprises, governments and wider society and economy. In 2019, two new indicators related to "robot technology" were introduced, and it is considered that digital knowledge, flexibility and artificial intelligence technology are essential to enhance digital competitiveness.

II. Development Prospect of Czech Manufacturing Industry

1. Development Advantages

According to the *Global Competitiveness Report 2019* published by the World Economic Forum, the Czech Republic ranked 29th among the 140 most competitive countries and regions in the world. The World Bank's *Doing Business* analyses and evaluates the business regulations and property rights protection of 190 economies in the world, and the result shows that the Czech Republic ranked 35th in 2019. According to the latest research report released by Cushman & Wakefield in 2020, the Czech Republic ranked 4th among the countries most suitable for manufacturing development in the world and came out 1st among European countries. Compared with other countries, the development advantages of the Czech manufacturing industry mainly lie in technological innovation, policy environment and integrated cost advantages.

(1) Advantages of Technological Innovation

Equipped with certain R&D capabilities and technological innovation advantages, Czech manufacturing industry enjoys a solid foundation for innovation and applied research with a rich high-skilled labor pool.

First of all, with a solid foundation for innovation and applied research, the Czech Republic stands a leading position in the cutting-edge scientific and technological fields such as driverless technology, life sciences and nanotechnology. Honeywell International, General Electric Airlines, BMW and many other large international companies have invested in building R&D centers in the Czech Republic. In 2017, the Czech Republic established 41 R&D centers with a total investment of RMB 21 billion yuan. For example, the Textile Engineering College of Technical University of Liberec (TUL) is committed to the research on the application and development of new materials such as nanotechnology in the field of clothing and technical textiles, developing composite structures containing inorganic fibers, nanoparticles and textile reinforcement materials, designing and evaluating intelligent textiles as well as improving and developing processing technologies for new materials, new energy and new transportation media in textiles. In addition, as Czech enterprises attach greater importance to R&D, they have expanded investment in R&D and gradually increased the proportion of R&D. Regular surveys conducted by the Czech Confederation of Industry show that more than 40% of industrial enterprises plan to increase investment. According to Eurostat data, the proportion of Czech R&D investment in GDP in 2018 was about 1.9%, slightly lower than the EU average (2.2%). The Czech Republic plans to elevate the proportion to 2.5% by 2025 and further to 3% by 2030.

Secondly, the Czech Republic is rich in high-skilled labor resources whose education level and quality are generally high. Judging from the quality of labor force, the Czech Republic possesses a group of high-quality and high-tech labor force. According to the data published by the Czech Statistical Office, the education level in the Czech Republic is generally divided into four categories, namely Grammar School, Secondary Technical Education, Higher Professional Education and University Education. As shown in Figure 3-4, the average Czech population has a relatively high level of education, with about 250,000 college-educated people. According to Eurostat data, the higher education penetration rate of Czech labor force aged 15 to 64 in 2019 was 21.6%. In addition, according to statistics, the overall education system of the Czech Republic ranks among the top 20 in the world while its per capita education level ranks the fourth in the world, and the average rate of higher education level ranks among the top ones in the European Union. On the whole, the Czech labor force is of high quality with abundant high-end technical talents, suitable for developing high-tech industries.

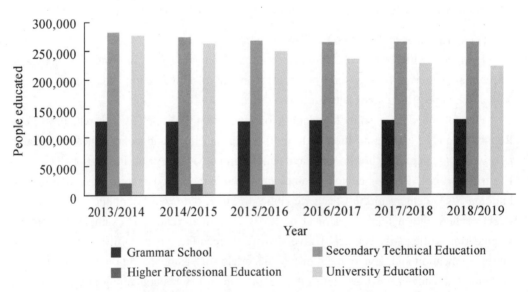

Figure 3-4   Distribution of Education Level of Czechs from 2013 to 2019

(**Source:** Czech Statistical Office)

(2) Policy Advantage

The Czech government encourages foreign investment, attaches importance to the promotion of foreign investment to Czech economy, and has policy advantages. In order to optimize the industrial structure, the Czech Republic has gradually adjusted its foreign investment policies and focus, and has successively introduced a series of preferential policies including taxation, employment, research and development, etc., to guide foreign investment into high-tech industries and emerging industries. According to the *World Investment Report 2020* released by UNCTAD, in 2019 the foreign investment flow in the Czech Republic was USD 7.577 billion, and by the end of 2019 the foreign investment stock in Czech was USD 170.682 billion.

In 1998, the Czech Republic implemented the Czech Investment Incentives Act to encourage foreign direct investment into the Czech Republic. Since then, the Czech government has revised the act in accordance with relevant EU regulations and changes in foreign investment structure, mainly to relax restrictions on foreign investment, adopt EU state support rules, reduce tax incentives and financial subsidies for manufacturing investment projects, and increase support for investment projects in technology centers and business support services. In May 2015, the newly revised Czech Investment Incentives Act strengthened the support for manufacturing, technology centers, business support service centers and strategic investors, and increased investment incentives. In order to improve the competitiveness of Czech industry and reduce the relevant budget, the Czech Republic began to implement the new Amendment of the Investment Incentives Act in September 2019, which mainly revised the application procedures, subsidy scope and subsidy conditions for investment incentives, so as to encourage projects that have high added value and can create more high-quality jobs. In the manufacturing sector, the new act requires that the wages of more than 80% employees in foreign-invested enterprises must meet the local average wage level, and must meet at least one of the following three conditions to be deemed to meet the high value-added conditions: 1) The proportion of college students in new jobs is not less than 10%; 2) R&D employees are not less than 2%; 3) The investment in R&D equipment shall not be less than 10% of the total investment. In addition, in terms of application procedures, it is stipulated that all applications for investment subsidies will be evaluated and approved by the Czech government. According to the principles of traditional advantages and development potential, the Czech government encourages foreign investment in high-tech manufacturing industries, such as electronics, electrical engineering, aerospace, high-end equipment manufacturing, high-tech automobile manufacturing, life sciences, nanotechnology, pharmaceuticals, biotechnology and medical equipment, renewable energy resources and clean technology.

According to the different stages of Czech economic development, the Czech government assesses the situation, advances with the times, and adjusts investment incentive policies in a timely manner. The government treats foreign investment and domestic enterprise investment equally and adopts the same preferential policies. With the support of national investment incentive policies and EU funds, Czech manufacturing industry is transforming and upgrading from primary production and assembly to advanced manufacturing industry with high technology and high added value by attracting and utilizing foreign capital.

(3) Integrated Cost Advantage

Compared with Western European countries, the Czech Republic has an obvious competitive advantage in terms of integrated cost. The Czech Republic is located in the "heartland" of Europe and has a strategic position as the center of a large European market; the transportation network is relatively developed, with convenient transportation by rail, highway, air and water, and convenient transportation with neighboring countries, making it an important transit hub of European transportation network. In 2019, the Czech Republic has 1,223 kilometers of highways and 2,628 kilometers of European high-speed networks, which connect with neighboring countries and radiate throughout Europe. It is the country with the highest density of transportation network in Central and Eastern Europe. Czech railways can lead to major European cities, with an actual operating mileage of about 9,564 kilometers and a density of 12 kilometers per 100 square kilometers. Czech aviation industry is developing rapidly, and it is connected with major European cities by air lines. Currently, there are 91 civil airports in the Czech Republic, including 7 international airports in Prague, Brno, Ostrava, Karlovy Vary and Pardubice, and 4 military airports in Čáslav and other cities. The Czech Republic is a landlocked country in Central Europe. There are no large ports or sea ports, but there are many small inland ports and docks, mainly located along the Elbe River in cities such as Děčín, Prague and Usti. Rotterdam and other large international ports can be conveniently reached from these inland ports. In addition, the Czech Republic has developed electric power and is a major power exporter in Europe; the communication industry has developed rapidly and has basically achieved networking.

2. Development Dilemma

Manufacturing industry is an important driving force of Czech economy, and has unique development advantages. But at the same time, Czech manufacturing industry is also facing many problems and challenges, mainly reflected in labor shortage, low labor productivity and decline in corporate profit margins.

(1) Labor Shortage

Like many European countries, the Czech Republic is also facing an increasingly serious labor crisis. Labor shortage, especially the shortage of professional and skilled workers, has aroused increasing concern of the Czech government and enterprises. Czech labor force is in short supply and cannot meet the demand of the job market. In some professional fields with large demand, the labor reserve is seriously insufficient, which leads to the imbalance between supply and demand in the labor market in the medium and long term. In 2018, 45% of Czech manufacturers listed labor shortage as one of the main factors limiting production, and the total number of job vacancies exceeded 300,000. The labor market shows obvious signs of overheating. Since April 2018, the number of job vacancies has begun to exceed the number of job seekers.

In terms of specific industries, the Czech Republic has insufficient number of fresh graduates that match the corresponding industries. For example, the automobile manufacturing industry has long lacked highly educated skilled workers. In 2018, there were about 20,000 job vacancies in the automobile manufacturing industry. The beer brewing industry is faced with the problem of lack of brewers. It usually takes several months or even a year to find a new brewer, so there are "flying brewers" who can take care of three to four micro breweries. For the textile and clothing industry, there is a severe shortage of new workers with textile-related education. On the one hand, there are not many young people interested in textile and clothing education in the Czech Republic. On the other hand, secondary education and apprenticeship education in textile and clothing fields are relatively weak. There are no other textile technical schools in the Czech Republic except Technical University of Liberec. In order to improve this situation, the Czech Republic initiated an agreement based on cooperation with regions, enterprises and schools, aimed at meeting the educational needs of textile enterprises in various regions.

The shortage of labor market is also reflected in the rapid growth of labor wages. In order to solve the problem of "difficult recruitment", Czech enterprises have to raise wages and try to attract workers from abroad. As shown in Figure 3-5, the growth rate of unit labor cost and average nominal wage show an upward trend. Although the growth rate declined slightly in 2019, it is still at a relatively high level of growth. Especially in the last two years, the average nominal wage and unit labor cost have increased much faster than labor productivity, which is not conducive to the sustainable development of Czech economy in the long run. In order to alleviate the problem of labor shortage, the Czech government has implemented a plan to hire workers from Ukraine in 2016. According to the statistics of the Czech Ministry of Labor and Social Affairs, there were 121,000 Ukrainians working in Czech by the end of 2018, accounting for 1/5 of the foreign employees. Since November 2019, the Czech Republic has increased the annual quota of Ukrainian workers from 19,600 to 40,000.

(2) Low Labor Productivity

Although Czech manufacturing industry has been growing in recent years, compared with Western European countries, its labor productivity still remains low, grows slowly and fluctuates greatly (see Figure 3-5). A comparison between the Czech Republic and Germany reveals that Czechs work longer hours than Germans, but their productivity and wages are lower than those of Germany. For example, in 2017, the hourly labor productivity of Czechs was USD 38, which was only 60% of the German labor productivity level; in 2018, the hourly labor productivity of Czechs was only 59% of that of Germans, and the productivity individual worker was 77% of that of Germans; in 2019, Czech labor force worked an average of 40 hours a week, higher than the EU average (37 hours) and Germany average (34.8 hours). In order to maintain the competitiveness of the manufacturing industry in the global economy, the Czech Republic urgently needs to continuously improve its labor productivity through automation and digitalization.

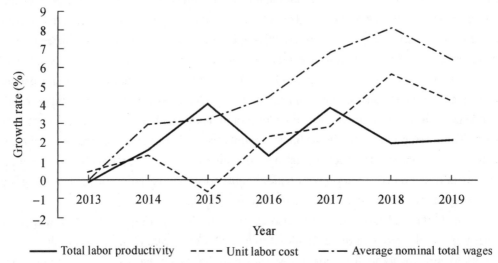

Figure 3-5   Trends of Czech Labor Productivity, Unit Labor Cost and
Average Nominal Wage Growth Rate from 2013 to 2019

(**Source:** Czech Statistical Office)

(3) Declining Corporate Profit Margins

The profits of Czech manufacturing enterprises have been squeezed by various factors, and profit margins have gradually declined. In addition to the increase in unit labor costs, other cost inputs, including electricity prices, raw materials and service costs, loan interest rates, are also increasing. These rising costs will easily become obstacles to the further development of enterprises. In the fierce market competition, enterprises often can't fully reflect higher costs into higher prices, and have to reduce profits. Due to the decline in profit margins, more and more manufacturing enterprises have to postpone or even reduce investment plans such as R&D.

3. Prospects for the Future

In the short term, affected by the epidemic, Czech economy was severely hampered by weak domestic and international demand, with manufacturing industry being the first to bear the brunt. The Manufacturing Purchasing Managers' Index (PMI) is a "physical examination chart" for measuring a country's manufacturing industry, and is regarded as a leading indicator to observe the economy. Among them, 50 is regarded as the boom-or-bust line, higher than 50 indicates economic prosperity and industry expansion; lower than 50 means the economic recession and industry shrinking. As shown in Figure 3-6, Czech manufacturing PMI fell to 49.7 in December 2018, which was the first time since August 2016 that it fell below the 50 threshold. Since then, the PMI has been below 50 and has gradually declined. In April 2020, Czech manufacturing PMI dropped to 35.1, the lowest level in the past decade. Indicators of production and new orders also experienced the largest decline since the financial crisis in 2009. The main reason is that due to the outbreak of the epidemic and the escalating anti-epidemic measures by the Czech government, the manufacturing demand has dropped sharply and a large number of enterprises have closed down. With the relaxation of control measures and the re-operation of enterprises, PMI continued to rebound until July, when it rose to 47, the highest in the past 16 months, but still below the 50 boom-or-bust line, and the prospect of manufacturing industry is still not optimistic. According to IHS Markit, Czech industrial production will fall by 10% in 2020.

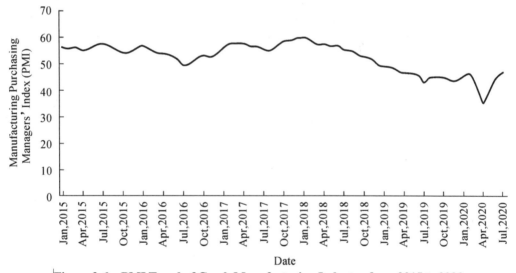

Figure 3-6   PMI Trend of Czech Manufacturing Industry from 2015 to 2020

(**Source:** IHS Markit)

The Czech Republic is a highly open economy. Its economic recovery cannot be independent of the global economy, and depends on the recovery of the global economy, especially the European Union. According to statistics, the Czech Republic ranks 17th in the Global Index of Economic Openness and 9th in the European Union. The high degree of economic openness means that the improvement of the international situation is vital to the

70

Development Report on Zhejiang-Czech Economic and Trade
Cooperation under the Framework of the Belt and Road Initiative (2020)

Czech Republic. The development of Czech manufacturing industry will largely depend on the international environment and domestic supporting measures. The COVID-19 epidemic will be the biggest threat to the current Czech manufacturing recovery. The escalation of trade protectionism, the Brexit, Sino-US relations, and European-American trade relations will increase uncertainty.

In the medium and long term, Czech manufacturing industry needs to tap new growth points and enhance its subsequent competitiveness. In the wake of the Fourth Industrial Revolution, innovation is extremely active; new technologies, new formats and new models such as artificial intelligence, cloud computing and big data are emerging one after another; the construction of a green, circular and low-carbon modern industrial system is accelerating. All these have brought about the restructuring of the global industrial division. In order to improve the competitiveness of the Czech Republic in the fourth industrial revolution, the Czech government officially approved the "Průmysl 4.0 (Industry 4.0) Initiative" in August 2016. In the initiative, it analyzed the development trend of Czech industry and the risks it might face in the future, and put forward corresponding suggestions. The initiative focused on areas such as data and communication facilities, education and skills, labor market and global supply chains. In February 2017, the Czech Ministry of Industry and Trade established the "Alliance Society 4.0" and formulated an action plan under the framework of the Industry 4.0. In September 2017, the Czech government officially approved the "Action Plan for Society 4.0", and listed education, labor, e-government, industry, entrepreneurship and competitiveness as the pillars of the plan. For the increasingly bottle-necked Czech manufacturing industry, Industry 4.0 can activate the labor market, improve the automation, intelligence and digitalization of the manufacturing industry, thus effectively alleviate the difficulties faced by Czech manufacturing industry, bring new opportunities to its development, and help the transformation and upgrading of Czech economy.

Acknowledgement

Development Report on Zhejiang-Czech Economic and Trade Cooperation under the Framework of the Belt and Road Initiative (2020) has been successfully released. Here we would like to thank all walks of life and all sectors of society for their help, guidance and support contributing to the release of this report.

In composing of this report, we received meticulous guidance from the Department of Commerce of Zhejiang Province. The Division of Foreign Economic Liaison, Division of Outbound Investment and Economic Cooperation, Division of General Management, Division of Foreign Trade Development, Foreign Trade Center and other relevant divisions under the Department of Commerce have provided full support and offered valuable suggestions for the revision of the report.

During the process of data collection, we received full cooperation and support from many enterprises such as CHINT Group, Dahua Technology, Wanxiang Group, Zhejiang Huajie Investment Development Co., Ltd., Hamaton Automotive Technology Co., Ltd. and so on.

Genuine appreciation goes to the colleagues of the Research Center and sincere gratitude goes to the teams of the English translation, Czech translation and external audit experts for their tireless efforts contributing to the successful publication of this report in Chinese, English and Czech versions at the same time.